The Joy of the Kingdom
Envisioning the Great Commission

James McReynolds
Minister of Joy to the World

Parson's Porch Books

The Joy of the Kingdom: Envisioning the Great Commission
ISBN: Softcover 978-1-951472-67-2
Copyright © 2020 by James McReynolds

All rights reserved. No part of this book may be reproduced or transmitted in any form or by any means, electronic or mechanical, including photocopying, recording, or by any information storage and retrieval system, without permission in writing from the publisher.

www.parsonsporch.com

Other Books by James McReynolds Published by Parson's Porch Books

The Spirituality of Joy: The Least Discussed Human Emotion

The Joy of Preaching: Encountering Jesus Through the Word of God

Dancing with God: A Theology of Joy

The Silence of the Church: The Spiritual Struggle with Sexuality

The Spirit of Joy Church

Joy Comes in the Mourning: Love Is Forever

The Joy of Prayer:

The Way to Intimacy with God

Envisioning the Great Commission: The Joy of the Kingdom

This book is dedicated to the churches where I served as a minister of joy, 1954-2020.

Woodlawn Baptist Church, Bristol, Tennessee
First Baptist Church, Knoxville, Tennessee
Summer missionary, Home Mission Board, Southern Baptist Convention
First Baptist Church, Ashland City, Tennessee
Daniel Boone Baptist Chapel, Gate City, Virginia
First Baptist Church, Hallsville, Missouri
Kingsville Christian Church, Kingsville, Missouri
Sunday School Board of the Southern Baptist Convention
Two Rivers Baptist Church, Nashville, Tennessee
Southminster United Presbyterian Church, Nashville, Tennessee
Citadel Park Baptist Chapel, Nashville, Tennessee
Lakewood Baptist Church, Nashville, Tennessee
East Side Baptist Church, Evansville, Indiana
Pilgrim Presbyterian Church, Cameron, Missouri
First Christian Church, Polo, Missouri
Kingston Christian Church, Kingston, Missouri
Zion United Church of Christ, Saint Joseph, Missouri
Camden Point Baptist Church, Camden Point, Missouri
Amazonia United Methodist Church, Amazonia, Missouri
First Presbyterian Church, Savannah, Missouri
First United Methodist Church, Savannah, Missouri
Saint John's United Church of Christ, Amazonia, Missouri
Christ Memorial Baptist Church, Saint Joseph, Missouri
Immanuel Lutheran Church, Saint Joseph, Missouri
Ridgecrest Baptist Church, Council Bluffs, Iowa
Calvary Baptist Church, Glenwood, Iowa
Hillcrest Baptist Church, Omaha, Nebraska
Westminster Baptist Chapel, Omaha, Nebraska
Shenandoah Presbyterian Church, Johnson City, Tennessee
Rich Valley United Methodist Church, Abingdon, Virginia
Washington Chapel United Methodist Church, Abingdon, Virginia
Brick United Methodist Church, Wytheville, Virginia
Fort Chiswell United Methodist Church, Fort Chiswell, Virginia
Harrison's Chapel United Methodist Church, Max Meadows, Virginia
First United Methodist Church, Max Meadows, Virginia
Locust Hill United Methodist Church, Locust Hill, Virginia
Graham's Forge United Methodist Church, Graham's Forge, Virginia

The Joy of the Kingdom

Saint Luke United Methodist Church, Bristol, Virginia
First Christian Church, Pawnee City, Nebraska
Saint Paul United Methodist Church, Elmwood, Nebraska
Chapel in the Elms, Elmwood, Nebraska
Faith Baptist Church, Nebraska City, Nebraska
First Presbyterian Church, Tecumseh, Nebraska
Elmwood Christian Church, Elmwood, Nebraska
Emmanuel Baptist Church, Hoenesbroek, The Netherlands
Saint Matthew Church, Lincoln, Nebraska
First Christian Church, Weeping Water, Nebraska
Spirit of Joy Christian Church, Elmwood, Nebraska

Contents

Dedication 7
Foreword 11
    Dr. John Killinger
Introduction 13
Chapter One 21
    Surprised By Joy 21
Chapter Two 29
    When Joy Wells Up 29
Chapter Three 39
    Joy In The Kingdom 39
Chapter Four 50
    The Biblical Concept Of Conversion 50
Chapter Five 60
    A Historical View Of Conversion 60
Chapter Six 73
    Ineffective Evangelism In The Post-Christian World 73
Chapter Eight 88
    Living The Vision Of God 88
Chapter Nine 106
    Sharing The Joy With Spiritual Formation
Chapter Ten 113
    New Vision With Creative Passion
Bibliography 123
Notes About The Author 133
Contact Information Visionquests For Joy International 135

Dedication

This book and all my books on joy are dedicated to those who embrace afresh vision that has evolved from life's journey. To those who have obeyed the Great Commission resulting in a new intimacy with God.

Jesus expects the church to keep proclaiming the Good News despite the pandemic of Covid-19 that kills millions every day. In the darkness and intensity, human lives are changed in unexpected ways. During this baffling pandemic, I am amazed how the disciples of 2020 shepherd new life in the fearful world. I dedicate this book to those envisioning the Great Commission with tireless tenderness and humanity do this impossible work.

The best book of 2020 reflects the pandemic of a hundred years earlier in1917-1918. Emma Donoghue published a novel in 2020, *The Pull of the Stars*. The novel is based in a Dublin hospital in Ireland. People are dying by the millions. The Irish government printed a sign for the people that could be placed in any city in America today.

STAY CLEAN, WARM AND WELL NOURISHED, BUT FORBEAR TO USE MORE THAN A FAIR SHARE OF FUEL AND FOOD. (Emma Donoghue, *The Pull of the Stars*, 2020, pp. 64, 293-294)

The influenza pandemic of 1918 killed more people than all that died in World War I. More than six per cent of humans were wiped out.

This book is also dedicated to health care workers who risk more than we can imagine and into whose hands we give ourselves.

The world is now in a holding pattern. All of us are living in a waiting zone. Flight is suspended. Previous routines are not possible. We are confined like a chrysalis in the birth sac yearning to fly like a butterfly. As people of faith, we are stalled from going outward, but we go inward. While we incubate a new way of being, God will sit with us, holding us close, giving us the gift of solace. God sees all we are going through with the pandemic and its deleterious effects

We fresh ways to do the Great Commission. We question and wonder about the next thing. Faithful pilgrims discover joy and resilient in these dark days. Our earthly journey is now new territory. We are called to let go of our certainties, and we are invited to embrace mystery.

Foreword
Dr. John Killinger

James McReynolds is one of the most faithful writers I know to see and exalt the importance of *Joy* in the whole matter of the Christian faith.

Jim sees what we often miss, that Jesus did not want his followers to be exemplars of solemnity and severity, as our churches often are, but practitioners and sowers of a great and mystical joy that emanates from the very throne of God. Jim's vision of the fire of joy should permeate everything we do as Christians.

I confess that I often forget this as I contend with the pressures of life. I need someone like Jim to remind me of its absolute centrality in our faith.

Think about it. It is easy, in a world filled with cares and responsibilities, to be overburdened by our duties and obligations, so that we often (if not usually) fail to exhibit the signal quality of exuberant happiness we were intended to enjoy.

Because this is our reality, Christianity is often regarded, by both insiders and outsiders, as somber, weighty, and difficult to manifest. This is not what God or Jesus ever intended for us. If we only think about the central thesis of our faith, that Jesus came and died to free us from our bondage to sin and death, we should be leaping and dancing with an irrepressible and unending happiness.

I know I fail at this. When I consider the weight of Jesus' command, I bear to carry Christianity's wonderful message to others, together with the difficulty I have in finding suitable expressions for that incomparable message, I usually become seriously leaden and impaired.

I try so hard to perform my duty to God and those who need to hear this message that I almost instantly lose my composure. I become serious and overwhelmed, and so burdened by the responsibility that I forget what a joyous and upbeat message it is, or really ought to be.

Thanks to you, minister of joy to the world, for your faithful proclamation of the absolute, inimitable joy of our faith, and the importance of our remembering it and embodying it in all our speech and actions as the incredibly gifted associates and advocates of our Lord Jesus Christ.

I mean it.

Dr. John Killinger, Warrenton, Virginia

Introduction

The Great Commission. Neither the words "great" nor "commission" are in the biblical text. Every Christian has an opportunity to participate in fulfillment of Jesus last command. From the beginning of my conversion, I thought that I should get a passport stamped and travel to share Christ's command in foreign nations.

Most people who follow Jesus in the Great Commission do so by supporting their local church, reaching non-Christians where they are located.

The apostle Paul reported in Romans 15:19, "From Jerusalem to Illyricum I fulfilled the ministry of the gospel of Christ." Paul did not preach to everyone from Jerusalem to Illyricum. This geographical region of the world was a vast area. Nobody could ever travel to every place. It has taken me 22 years just to complete my ministry to the communities in Nebraska. Paul did not have the technology was not that Paul had technology to share his passion with every single city. This was his dream, his vision.

For one thing Paul established churches. Paul considered his part in the Great Commission was fulfilled when the local churches were solidly planted. He had preached in the major communities between the two geographical cities on the way. Whenever Paul planted a church, that body of Christ accepted the responsibility for sharing the faith in the region surrounding it.

A church is not healthy unless specific attention is given to Great Commission. We who are called must redefine success so that it includes church planting. For a local congregation to have life, it must exist for ventures outside of itself. Sometimes our huge mega churches refuse to reproduce themselves. They do not want to pay the cost involved.

Too many churches enjoy numerical growth simply from Christians transferring from one church to another.

Churches are struggling to change how they do evangelism. *Faith-Sharing* by Eddie Fox and George Morris, *Pastoral Evangelism* by Samuel Southard, *Proclaiming the Great Commission* by Claude Payne and Hamilton Beasley, and *Unbinding the Gospel* by Martha Reese are insightful books. Conversion and evangelism have been misunderstood. Churches are unable to reach individuals not socialized in the Christian faith by family members or with attendance in the education and worship provided.

The landscape of most communities has move from Christian to post-Christian. This book is an attempt to reassess the adequacy of outreach practices. There is an urgent need to reevaluate how churches conceive the conversion process. They need to understand the sociological spaces their vision of faith has established. Insights are needed that equips the now dying congregations to reach people from new strategies and a broad spectrum.

That predicament shows the urgent need to get a clear understanding of what Scripture teaches regarding conversion. In a historical overview of how conversion has been understood. The reader will consider how modern evangelism shapes the concept of conversion and the practice of evangelism with a need to conceive of conversion as a process, not an instantaneous event.

In 2020, the 300th anniversary of the Christmas carol, "Joy to the World. "That theme has been sustained through the history of Christianity. Life has not changed for most people. Disappointment and disrespect of Christian character, the organized church, and the lack of joy exceed expectations.

The Great Commission of Jesus the Christ has been lost as essential to Christian faith. The church has become impoverished. With a declining membership, the church is isolated from the world it seeks to bring the joy of salvation.

A starting point is to acknowledge what already works, embracing the best of what has proven effective. This must be more than an enhancement of the status quo. The church must adapt to meet the circumstances and challenges in a world rapidly changing. Throughout the historical eras, the Holy Spirit has moved among the faithful when a loss of evangelistic focus has weakened the Body of Christ and has brought division, hate, pride, and entitlement. A renewed commitment and understanding of the biblical and historic gospel are the key to finding the keys of the kingdom.

When the word "salvation" is spoken of anywhere, it means entry into heaven when one dies. Being "saved" is to be counted by God with people who will be admitted at death. Using those words keeps people from understanding the sense of deliverance. This loss results from the age-old obsession with forgiveness of sins. Control over forgiveness is the foundation for successful "evangelism" in many congregations. If the understanding of forgiveness is the profession of belief, then we have a consumer view of Christian faith. Joy and the other fruit of the Spirit are conceived by Paul as "fruit of light in all that is good and right and true." Ephesians 5:9. The fruit is the inner character. It is the outcome of genuine spiritual formation.

Paul described the difference between human wisdom and the wisdom of God. Human logic was a spiritual barrier. The church needed to repudiate that wisdom that appealed to the carnal nature. Paul used divine wisdom in evangelism. He told the Corinthians that effective evangelism included four things. Read I Corinthians 2:1-5. Paul's evangelism did not rely on a form. He noted the effectiveness of language. He admitted he did not have excellency of speech when he preached. He also did not have the skill of argumentation. Paul did not rely on worldly wisdom. During times of unsettled faith, skepticism, and mere curious speculation, the church invites and shapes its own preachers. People who are immature believers will go from church to church looking for a preacher who satisfies them.

Their concept of attractive preaching is not sound biblical exposition. They want to hear interesting suggestions and stories based on the preacher's personal theology. They are not wanting a word from God to believe, but a word for church members to consider. I heard the story about a Southern Baptist church that had beautiful stained-glass windows. The window just behind the pulpit depicted Jesus hanging on the cross. That day, the guest preacher was shorter than the pastor. A young boy listened for a few minutes. He then asked his mom, "Where is the man who usually stands there so we can't see Jesus?"

The content of Paul's evangelism was simple and clear. He preached "Jesus Christ and He crucified." Paul presented the person of Jesus, including his deity and humanity. Read Acts 18:4-5. His preaching conveyed spiritual, biblical, and logical arguments. Paul had no interest in discussions about human insights. His evangelistic preaching proclaimed nothing but Jesus Christ. His preaching content never viewed Jesus as simply a perfect teacher or the example of what a perfect man was like. His homiletic foundation was Jesus as the Savior.

This is the paradox of evangelism. The paradox is the preaching a crucified Christ, which has the power and wisdom that no human eloquence possesses. It is the power and wisdom of God.

Finding the joy of the kingdom means to humbly recognize our frailty. We come as human to human, expecting that the words we speak will convert souls. Our words we speak are considered as "weak." Jesus gave the Great Commission, an awesome responsibility as John Killinger noted in the forward to this book.

Paul said he came in the demonstration of the power of God. The gospel gripped its hearers and brought conversion. This is the wisdom of God in evangelism. The Spirits power does not depend upon the eloquence of the preacher or in the cleverness of her argument.

My model of salvation is confidence in Jesus Christ, the whole person, not just one part of what he said and did. Salvation delivers the disciple into life in the kingdom of God. That is a process of inner transformation, not the condition for getting into heaven. Deliverance will be, as communities used to sing in revivals, "Be of sin the double cure, save from wrath and make me pure." Inclusiveness in the kingdom of God is the grace of rooted in spiritual formation in Christ.

The role of the church is not to conceive a demand for spiritual experiences. The needed proclamation is to explain the demand that already exists. Evangelistic activities are answers to a plea that is unstated. Scriptures reveal evangelism as responsive, not intrusive. To reject evangelism is to ignore the hope of alienated individuals who really want a relationship with God, giving them a meaning and life purpose. Conversion is a process. It involves interaction with other humans and God who uses us to carry out the divine work. Conversion is not an event, but a way of life that leads to deeper and intimate relationships with God.

Converted into the kingdom of God brings dedication and commitment. The Bible and church history enhance a community of wisdom. That joy and wisdom contains thousands of years of knowledge about the ways God has acted with God's children. Spirituality is not about doing what one desires but doing the plans of God. Conversion is not a painless process. The pain of turning from sin as pleasure and abandoning the false gods of greed, power, and entitlement. This is nothing in comparison to the joy of embracing a real God. The conversion experience brings unification of the soul to its creator, a realignment of individual will with God's will. Conversion is a rejoining of the beloved child with its Parent.

Evangelism is faith carried out into the world. The actions of Jesus were concerned with the kingdom in the world now and to come. Most religious fundamentalism gives a concrete, absolute structure that their followers find appealing, but over time is restricting with rigid answers. Non-fundamentalists discredit the language of the church, rejecting the resurrection and rejecting the role of God in human lives.

Communication of the Gospel through preaching, teaching, counseling, writing, newsletters, and conversation needs to express the faith in language that is secular enough to be understood by the unchurched, and theological enough to transform lives. The Word of God is the story of transformations. Prayerfully, the church can be God's agent with a passion for making disciples. We are the Ministers of Joy to the World. The choice is between hoarding the joy of salvation and sharing it with the world. Cultural environment can help or hinder. Cultivating self-control and courage is made more difficult in a society given over to sensuality. This makes it even harder to live in Christ in the current culture context. The deeper discipline, constant prayer, and dependence and obedience to the Holy Spirit, the more we can bring changes in culture, rather than being content with shielding ourselves, consistently, freely, and joyously. We are allowed what we call "free will" to choose to be what we are. It is up to us. Citizens of the kingdom of joy do not live in a closed circle. Our fellow kingdom people empower us to know qualities that we never knew existed.

Politicians in the world culture as well as church culture lack courage making a travesty of justice. Think of Pontius Pilate and his concept of justice. He said, "I could find no substance to any of the charges you bring against him, so I will scourge him." This frightening logic is the root of cowardness, not courage. Lobbyists, rich people, lustful people, and those that use their earthly beauty lure politicians and church controllers. A sample case is found in the New Testament story of Herodias. In her passionate lust, she demanded the head of John the Baptist because he had the temerity to insist that she change her ways.

As I began to share the manuscript with friends and the folks active in my new church plant, Spirit of Joy Christian Church. Some said they thought this book might be an ecclesiastical and political failure. I responded that I want to move the talk to action. My hope is that the church will recover from the unmitigated decline. The world's need of the Good News is more than any other time in history. I have looked the church straight in its eye. God is always doing new things. Just as the political climate, church people are extremely defensive about protecting the old order. I was banned from Facebook after my thoughts about the Donald Trump administration. He has used the old traditional evangelicals to keep his power. My writing is not an attack on the systems that put in power narcissistic, self-centered, and powerful white people. We care for our own, families first. The American climate is like the divisions that led to the Civil War. Churches started the political and cultural divisions at least twenty years before that war started in South Carolina in 1861. The Southern Baptist Convention was created in a split with the Northern Baptist Convention (now American Baptist Churches in the USA) in 1845. Denominations formed northern and southern branches including Presbyterians and Methodists.

My goal is to ignite an alternation from the present systems of doing church. Fulfillment of the Great Commission depends on change. It means living in God's vision, if we are to continue to have a part in expanding God's kingdom and not our own. There is an excitement as the Body of Christ rediscovers the power of the Good News.

John Killinger discusses the radical changes taking place in understanding of the concept of salvation with the globalization of culture and with the internet and miracles in communication. He challenges the present-day followers of Jesus to rethink church and Christianity.

Killinger's most recent insights are found in his book, *Outgrowing Church*. As my friend and mentor, he suggests that some of the problem is that so many are drifting away from churches. They have gone beyond the thinking, the openness and concepts of the cultural church. People no longer feel it adequate as a social structure for the celebration of faith.

In attempts to find and know God in Jesus within the emerging culture, they strike out on their own. They abandon the nationally favored church and its exclusion of those who are not in line with them. They can gather in a community without the baggage of the tradition institution. Traditions are a common part of our lives. They can be effective. They can be good. Not all traditions are wrong. Sometimes traditions can take the joy out of life. I often hear that if people are too religious. Those who hold onto only the old traditions, they will not be able to be led by the Holy Spirit and enjoy an intimate relationship to God.

When God directs us to change, we step into the joy of salvation. When God asks us to change, it means God has something better to give us. God promises that the plan is of sheer joy. Every time I experience it, I drop my fruits like a ripe tree. Killinger is not merely a critic but a critical lover, who has inside lived with the fruit of the Spirit.

This is the book I was born to write. Aspiring writers often speak of the one book churning inside their soul. In the videos in my mind, the spiritual telescope was turned around. I have prayed and cried thinking about how much more I could have done with my life.

Much of a writer's life is sent in solitude, especially during this virus endemic. I am just not able to keep on traveling and doing what I call spiritual vision quests. I read, study, discuss the possibilities of my published work with friends and family. I hammer out chapters at the computer. My long-time mentor who has graciously written forwards, giving me thoughtful feedback and encouragement. Thanks to the Parson's Porch Books, my publisher, this book is now complete. Thank you for getting it. I do pray that you are as eager to begin reading as I am to have written it by the grace of God.

I am running the last lap in my earthly journey. God tells me that my Lord knew me before I was born. Each year, I have become more intimate with God through prayer. Every word I preach and teach, every word I write comes from the Christ who lives in my inner soul. Sometimes I will speak wise and inspiring words that I had not imagine saying. I believe that at those times, Christ Jesus is speaking through me.

In these years of surrender to the Holy Spirit, miracles have happened. I have been surprised by joy beyond my wildest imagination. The torch of joy burns with passion inside and outside in my physical body and my eternal body.

I appreciate the hundreds of expressions of gratitude for my sharing the Great Commission. Kay Koch, an energetic woman, who followed me as she replaced me as moderator for the Nebraska region of the Christian Church (Disciples of Christ) in the United States and Canada, was among those writing a note.

Kay's note is in my treasure collection: "You have touched so many lives and I want to thank you for touching mine. Your joy will continue on in my life and I will try to instill this same joy into others as well."

Paul wrote in II Corinthians 3:18, "We all, with open face beholding as in a glass the glory of the Lord, are changed into the same image from glory to glory."

I shall not stop or slow down on my last life lap. I remain open to go into the world sharing the joy of salvation. During my transformation God has given me a gift of wisdom. I am fully committed to promoting joy and inspiring others to make the world a more joyful place.

Finding and sharing joy, no matter your age, helps to brighten someone's day and to improve spiritual, physical, mental health. We miss the pre-pandemic life when we could know the physical intimacy of a hug during Covid-19.

When the day arrives and I go on to the Next Place, I would like my tombstone to read: Minister of Joy to the World.

"A joyful heart is the normal result of a heart burning with love. She gives most who gives with joy."

-Mother Teresa

Chapter One
Surprised by Joy

Surprised by Joy was the first book I read in preparation for a class on the Theology of Joy taught by Chris Meadows at Vanderbilt Divinity School's. Lewis of Oxford University wrote of his conversion to Christ. Lewis 'wonderful title stimulates the time any person receives salvation in Jesus. After that class, I decided to poke around the scholarly atmosphere searching for writings about joy. At the time there were few writings about joy.

William James defined conversion as "a confused person, and consciously wrong, inferior, and unhappy, becomes unified and consciously right, superior and happy, in consequence of its firmer hold upon religious realities." (David A. Leeming, *Encyclopedia of Psychology and Religion*, pp. 155-156.) Joy has been omitted in intellectual circles. When I studied at Carson-Newman, I graduated *magna cum laude*, but I made C's in introduction to biology, chemistry, and physical sciences. In those days, many non-science majors took nuclear physics and astronomy courses from an instructor who was known to give all A's in his classes. I heard that his classes were fun and did not require what the science classes did. I found more joy enhancement in psychology courses.

I read *Human Emotions* by Carol Izard. She devoted chapter 16 to the emotion joy. Joy has been the least studied human emotions. I consulted with the new positive psychology movement at the University of Pennsylvania, an Ivy League school in Philadelphia. The scholars there have neglected a systematic study of joy. The word joy was rarely mentioned until Yale University Divinity School received a Templeton grant to focus on joy for five years.

Joy is vital to well-being. Theologians such as Chris Matthews, who taught a doctoral course on the theology of joy at Vanderbilt, got me hooked on as I found no serious discussion about human flourishing is possible without considering the nature of joy and its place. Contributing to the current problems with evangelism, discipleship, and conversion is the fact that joy has all but disappeared from preaching, teaching, and theological reflection. In my designation of my ministry as the Minister of Joy to the World in Vision Quests for joy, I have realized that we cannot understand human beings unless we understand joy. When my audiences get hooked, they are eager to share their experiences of joy. I have books of journals filled with thousands of testimonies about joy, where their souls are opened, giving their existence a fluidity, a sense of calm and easiness. No wonder churched believers cannot conceive of joy, how it occurs, how it changes lives, and how it is sustained or thwarted.

Joy is central to spiritual formation and always has been. It is ingrained into the spiritual fabric of spiritual reality that transcends traditions. Faith is a human emotion. It is not an exclusive experience for only confessing Christians. Disciplines enable us to do without direct effort. Solitude and silence, study and worship, fasting and frugality, service and submission and integral parts of spiritual formation. The gifts of the Spirit are supernatural abilities that are distributed to believers so all other believers can benefit. Without these gifts, fruit will not be sustained. Joy emanates from the disciplines of philosophy and theology. Seekers throughout history have cited joy as essential to human life and well-being. Nobody can have too much joy. Joy must be recognized as a positive emotion which bears on behavior and action for human flourishing. If joy is a synonym for happiness, the efforts to kindle a science of joy are redundant. There are levels of happiness.

I conceive happiness as containing guilt, anger, anxiety, fear, as well as joy. Happiness might be showing that one enjoys living even if every day is not filled with joy. Tradition congregations give vague suggestions on joy. There are few books and sermons on the connection between emotion and ethics. Most descriptions of joy state that joy is a response to something perceived as good or miraculous such as the birth of a child, a wedding, a graduation, or a healing. In some of the stories that have been shared with me, the joy experienced involved a single event or a transient state. Congregations and denominations would be wise to listen to those trained in both theology and psychology. These issues are too big to fit neatly into any disciplinary box. Joy matters. Like I wrote in my book on the joy of prayer to find intimacy with God, we need to do more than simply talking about it or writing about it. "The joy of the Lord" must be experienced. Part of being a disciple is to learn how to be joyful, that joy come with human development. The human capacity for joy is locked in from the beginning. My grandson Ethan gave me a colorful picture that has the words, "Find joy on your journey."

People know joy when they experience it. And they know when they lose the capacity for joy.

Every moment of our lives is intertwined whether we realize it or not. Videos of surprising times of joy during our life journeys reveal when and why and how we stumbled into joy. For more than 50 years, I have been writing about joy. There is ecstatic joy and sorrow in writing my life. Notes of joy are softly played as I think of the joy of salvation.

Our conversations focus on emotion. People ask, "How are you?" We might just say, "Fine and you?" Those close to us talk about things that upset us, what saddens us, and what brings joy. Culture and tradition taught us that emotions are irrational, a sign of weakness, childish, and unreliable. Negative emotions overtake us and those we love. A welcome alternative to the stormy and tumultuous culture is when we hear a cool sphere of reason.

As a retired ordained minister, I attend a group of other retired ministers. We often look back on our lives. We are constantly sharing our moments of respite. Awareness of our emotions and response to each other's plight and the coping mechanisms we use to accept things we cannot change. My daughter Linda was born in Nashville Memorial Hospital. My ex-wife Nancy carried our joy treasure out the front door of the hospital. A summer soft wind was felt by the three of us. I saw a faint smile in Linda's lips for the first time. Her smile carried wisdom beyond her years, as if she were telling us, "Your soul is older, by I know things you do not." She and her best friend Allison shared sounds of innocent, unselfconscious, unabashed laughter. Nancy and I recorded that playing time as a permanent record of joy.

Linda taught me how to play again in my joy of play, in my play of joy. I also found this in my grandson Ethan in playing with him and his toys, sharing our imagination as sparks begin to fly, and reading books as he nestled in my arms. And I know all realized that life is good. And there is abundant joy in that revelation. And in my moments of real life, I have touched joy, invited it in, and caressed in all my life and ministry.

During these final years of my life journey, I have laughed more often. I continue to feel sudden surges of joy, or discovery, of wonder. Not using the taboo-word or the r-word, my flashes of energy comes from meeting someone who sees things differently, from writing words into being, from meeting young students and helping them walk toward their best possibilities. I feel more delight in the uninhibited presence of children. Part of my soul anticipates all life coming together in a shimmer, in a splash, in a burst, in an earthquake or a little soft voice. "Evangelism" and "revival" are words used frequently in my quest. "Reap what you sow" was a frequent subject of sermons during "revivals" in my boyhood. In my times of listening to God in prayer, I believe I can sow more seeds of joy into my life, and to feel the joy of salvation, wholeness, more. I do want to continue writing joy and "joying" my writing for as long as I possibly can.

I have a sense that our youth are being formed into a false faith. Some believe that a God exists who created and orders the world and watches over human life. They believe God wants people to be nice, fair, and good to each other as taught in the Bible and in world religious. The central goal for life is to be happy and to feel good about oneself. Many ministers fit in to this imposter faith. Most of my ministry has been in evangelical churches, Youth for Christ and college rallies. I attended a Baptist college, a Southern Baptist seminary, a university divinity school, and international universities. I have and continue to believe that a converted disciple has responded to Jesus' call on life, who has left their old life behind, put on Christ, conformed to the image of Christ, for the sake of others in the world, extending Jesus' ministry, totally committed to the person and destiny of Jesus, abide intimately with God, bear fruit by loving others and obeying Jesus' commands.

This brings wholeness and glorious transformation, which is the result of Jesus' teaching, preaching, and healing. By changing the lives of individuals, Jesus changed the society in the world. Loving others is the Great Commandment to love God will all the heart, and to love the neighbor as one loves oneself. Evangelism is grounded in love. It is for the lost, the needy, the suffering of those unconverted. The means are discipleship and baptism.

As Christians we bask in the glow of joy and grace. Giving a blessing or grace depends on circumstances, temperament, mood, or out of our willingness. Bestowing grace is a part of God's divine vision and passionate love. "Amazing Grace" has been recorded the greatest number of times and by the greatest number of musicians in history. The hymn was written by John Newton, a slave trader. The joy of salvation springs from the love of God. Grace declares us worthy even though we are not. Human grace does not find us worthy or to see past unattractive behavior. Forgiven people are full of joy and they feel secure in divine acceptance. If we are supremely confident in our salvation in Christ, then we have a true and authentic joy. It is apparent to all who meet us. Joy is infectious oozing out a welcoming heart and spirit. When we experience such joy, we want others to experience the same joy. The joy of the Lord has characteristics that are real.

Authentic joy does not wane and wax with our life circumstances. People tend to associate the miracles of joy with what is happening. Joy is deeper than mere sentiment. Joy takes on an unbelievable calming and confidence. Joy does not ebb and flow with the events in our lives. "The joy of the Lord" is just that as joy is God's gift to us. This joy finds its source in God and in God alone. How can one capture joyful memories, so that these sweet times surprise us.at any moment in your lifetime? During the last McReynolds family reunion, when my brother David was alive, we sang, "A million tomorrows may all pass away, unless I forget the joys that are mine today." In my life's joys video, I am reminded to slow down and notice the joy times. We took scores of photographs that remain in a book to capture these moments. We can capture joyful core memories by taking a snapshot of a moment in the head. This is how we can hold on to our joy moments. Write in a journal those big and little moments of joy. That memory is then experienced again at any time. We never know when joy will come as a surprise. Memories become eternal. We cannot control when joy happens.

"Have your heart right with Christ, and Christ will visit you often, so turn weekdays into Sundays, meals into sacraments, home into temples, and earth into heaven," Charles Haddon Spurgeon said. The English pastor also said, "The grace of the spirit comes only from heaven, and it lights up the whole bodily presence. "Anny Crosby, the hymn writer, was devout from her childhood. On November 20, 1850, she had a dramatic conversion during a Methodist revival. "My very soul was flooded with celestial light. I danced with joy. The Lord had planted a star in my life and no cloud ever obscured its light." She spent several days each week in the missions of the bowery district of New York.

Crosby was always eager to hear any reports regarding any conversions that would be reported from the use of her hymns. She continued in prayer that God would allow her to be the means of leasing millions to Christ during her lifetime. She always had a dep love for children. Even in her old age when asked to speak in a church worship, she always included a children's sermon. She was partial to the Methodists, but she served with any Christian body. She enjoyed hearing Phillips Brooks in Boston and Henry Ward Beecher at Plymouth Congregational Church in Brooklyn. Fanny said, "Grace, the outward expression of the inward harmony of the soul." (William J. Reynolds, *Hymns of Our Faith: A Handbook for the Baptist Hymnal*, 1976, 176-182.This joy is more solid and stable than the rising sun. Because joy comes as an act of God, our unshakable rock, we and know the true source of joy will never be shaken. Read Psalm 18:2. No matter what happens we will never live without hope. When a moment of joy surprises us with that feeling of joy, look around. Smell the smells. Hear the sounds. See the scene. Notice the azure sky. Feel the temperature. Feel the blowing breeze. Close the eyes. Breathe.

Joy is not found in immediate gratification. Joy enables to push past the temporary pleasures. Everywhere we turn, wherever we go, whatever is going on, however skeptical we are, the promise of God's joy is held out to us in such deepness beyond human understanding.

C.S. Lewis wrote, "We are half-hearted creatures, fooling about with a drink and sex and ambition when infinite joy can be ours, like an ignorant child who wants to go on making mud pies in a slum because he cannot imagine what is meant by the offer of a holiday at the sea. We are far too easily pleased. "Demonstrating joy in difficult times such as the current disease, the Covid-19, kills millions all around the world, makes a difference for those living in the kingdom of God. Those outward signs of faith, such as joy, are ultimately dependent on the firmness of our foundation. Our calling is accomplished at the heart level. Our faithful work might not be as immediately gratifying as focusing on the beauty and pleasures on the surface. The Holy Spirit will guide you with joy strength. Long before our joy is expressed outwardly, it is formed inwardly through hope, faith, and love. His joy is unshakable.

Our lives reflect the joy of the gospel. This joy brings a reputation of a joyous designation that points to Christ. This designation is an invitation for all people in your circle to embrace what they now have. Remember what we deserve. One enemy or roadblock to joy is entitlement. That occurs a lot in a nation with a history of greed, injustice, and evil when especially rich and white skinned people foster the false idea that they deserve something better than the life situations in which we find ourselves. Remember what we do have. Comparison will rob us of joy. We covet what others have and even vote in greed for the status quo to continue. We make no room to share joy.

God paid a huge price for salvation. God did not rescue us with silver or gold. Those who love money and what money can give are living in the root of all evil. God's salvation was something more valuable. We do not boast with words of entitlement. In God's joy, our souls burn white hot with joy for the glory of the Lamb that was slain. One of the most meaningful Visionquests for Joy was held in the summer of 1992 at the First Presbyterian Church in Bristol, Tennessee's. Lewis reminded us that "joy is the serious business of heaven." Lewis also said, "Joy is never in our power and pleasure often is." Some thoughts shared included, "I think joy has a spiritual quality." Another was: "I feel joy when I am with certain people. With my best friends and family, I have that deep feeling of deep, no matter when and why we get together."

A proud young mother said, "I will never forget feeling such a deep sense of joy when I watched my daughter dance and play the piano. Maybe my joy is connected to pride. I believe joy is connected to that."

A schoolteacher related, "I think joy is connected to gratitude. When I am grateful, I know I feel joy at the same time." Our time together was exciting. Participants shared moments of joy, most connected to having a fresh awareness of an expanded sense of the meaning of life. Some said, "This is really important in connection with the joy of salvation." A former classmate of mine at Tennessee High School in Bristol shared that she had a deep joy at her mother's deathbed. The family prayed in a circle around her mother. She died peacefully with a smile. They were all deeply grieved, but she said she felt a profound sense of joy.

Joy. It is a short but powerful word. At each of my "revivals," I ask those who attend to share a moment of joy from their lives. Joy is like a deep abiding. The dictionary defines joy as "the emotion evoked by well-being, success, or good fortune or by the prospect of possessing what one desires." My definition is so much different. Joy is a major part of conversion. A joy feeling comes from deep within the soul and it is a gift of the Holy Spirit.

Joy is certainly one of our human emotions. Joy is a feeling. It is a knowing that life's journey derives from the confident abiding in the vine. Read John 15. Joy brings the future expectation that everything in life and death will be an eternal vision.

As I experience "the joy of the Lord" for myself, I want to share this everlasting joy with others. God is love. God is good. Joy rises from the confident assurance of that. It is impossible to separate joy from the Great Commission.

Joy is like a kiss. We must share it to enjoy it. Obedience to Jesus' commission is sharing a story that made you smile. It is walking by a stranger and flashing a smile. It is watching somebody dig for needed change and giving some of your own to cover their purchase. Research on spirituality and Christian conversion proves that sharing is a powerful way to have a joy. Sharing is the basic background for all human relationships and civilizations. Not only does sharing bring us joy, but it also teaches the importance of taking care of others. In many cultures, especially in Asian countries, it is common to share your home with your elders.

When we serve others, we serve ourselves. We do not think that I will help others. Think, I shall help my own world, because this is the source of joy. When we treat others in unkindness, we receive unkindness in return. And our own souls will grow shriveled and dry.

A few years back, my grandson Alex loved to know the history of football. Alex admired my encyclopedia of football and my life collection of every game ever played. Unhesitatingly, I gave it to him. One of my friends sked me, "Weren't you just a little bit sorry?" I replied, "Never for a moment, for sharing with such a fine boy expanded my own joy."

My own model brings the result as joy, as God says to the faithful, "Well done, good and faithful servant. Enter into the joy of your master."

"To get the full value of joy you must have someone to divide it with."
–Mark Twain

Chapter Two
WHEN JOY WELLS UP

The kingdom of heaven starts from the joy of God. Our Father finds joy in taking us into the kingdom. Read Luke 12:32-40. Joy wells up in pleasure, satisfaction, and contentment in this spiritual kingdom. Jesus taught us to pray that the kingdom would come. Bringing an enlightening concept of salvation causes us to know that the kingdom begins from the joy of God as a gift beyond fear. Imagine that your life is in danger from evil attackers who are coming after you relentlessly. The attackers do not stop or slow down. They are harmed with deadly weapons designed to inflict maximum injury, pain, and ultimately death. Imagine that you are cornered with no place to escape. All you can do is to wait for the inevitable to happen.

Now imagine that somebody steps out of nowhere, rescues you, and takes down the attackers. How do you feel toward that strong person who saved your life? Most of us would respond with sobs of joy. We would be so completely overwhelmed with joy that we would keep weeping. We would embrace the rescuer and say, "Thank you, thank you, thank you." We would never forget that person, never forget that moment, never lose that joy. This is what happens when someone is converted to Christ Jesus. God delivers us from sin and death. Joy naturally follows. Christianity without joy is not Christianity.

Marianne Williamson speaks to my soul, "When we are centered on joy, we attain our wisdom." When I was sharing my concepts of joy in South Korea, I was told that when a person turns 70, they become a new baby. The final years of life are the best years for joy.

At the Armstrong-Browning Library at Baylor University, I enjoyed a word from Robert Browning, "How good is man's life, the mere living. How fit to employ all the heart and the soul and the senses forever in joy."

Joy comes from experiencing the mercy of God. The maintenance of joy continues through a regular remembrance of the mercy from God. Joy is a radical deliverance from death. No wonder that there is such eruptive joy in heaven when a sinner repents. Angels singing, those living in heaven smiling is a picture of a person who hears the gospel, realizes the life he has live has broken God's laws, and makes up his mind that he will leave that old miserable life and live for God in the kingdom forever. His human nature changes and his name is written in the Lamb's Book of Life. God and the angels become so excited when this mighty miracle takes place in the life of a human that heaven stops everything to rejoice.

Helen Keller lived a challenging life. She said, "Joy is the holy fire that keeps our purpose warm and our intelligence aglow."

Citizens of the kingdom are people full of responsibility, not someone who lives under some other sort of regime. Without fear and in the spirit of joy, we live with righteousness. The kingdom arrives. The things that had seemed impossible become possible. Sharing good news provides us with an extra portion of joy.

I am so under conviction by the lack of positive excitement I see in churches when a sinner is saved. People yawn and cover their mouths as if nothing really happened. Christians should shout, yell, and jump in joy. Angels live in the breathtaking presence of God. They regularly see God's wonders that are beyond imagination.

Joy wells up because of the fruit we bear. This creates in us an atmosphere we live in. Salvation is God's making us to be new creatures created in Jesus. God has blessed us with spiritual blessings. Read Galatians 5:16-24.

We are branches of the vine. Read Colossians 1:9-17. In John 15:4-11, John writes about the nature of God's love as we connect with God intimately. Peter connects true faith in I Peter 1:3-12. This filling with joy is special. For joy wells up because this joy comes from God, from Jesus, and the Holy Spirit.

Ellen G. White, a leader in the Seventh-Day Adventist movement, said, "It is the chief joy of all holy beings to witness the joy and happiness of those around them."

William Tyndale was a passionate man who translated the scriptures into English. He said that salvation makes a person glad as he or she dances, sings, and leaps for joy. Tyndale stressed that the free grace and total forgiveness in Christ is the base of all joy and comfort.

We who search for God encounter difficult days. We see death and suffering all around us with the pandemic virus, wars, accidents, and the fragile realities of living on earth today. In the worst circumstances the work of Jesus makes it possible for us to be in joy. God is on our side. God walks with us in every circumstance of life.

In my book *Joy Comes in the Mourning: Love Is Forever*, I was writing of the anticipation of joy beyond this life's journey. My youngest brother David died last year. He, like me, was baptized in the Woodlawn Baptist Church in Bristol, Tennessee. He knew the gift of forgiveness. He has now come face to face with Jesus. His joy is complete. There is no more pain, no suffering, no regrets. Underneath all suffering and trials, we have a robust joy because our sins have been forgiven and our relationship with God is restored. Salvation includes the oil of joy for mourning, the garment of praise for the spirit of heaviness. This joy is real, deep, pure, and eternal.

Scientists have concluded that authentic conversions do not show a mere fantasy. They are a true way of perception and understanding of reality. The soul meets something real. Their research shows this connection does not belong to the world of senses that people experience. The person who knows this transformation is led outside toward encounters deeper dimensions of reality. Read Psalm 8:3. "From the lips of children and infants, you, Lord have called forth your praise."

Ecstatic conversion includes partial suspension of human consciousness. This supernatural ecstasy occurs in the prophetic or mystical form. It is grace given for free. It is not just the fruit of spiritual development. God's activity is important. God is offering to act inside a human soul. Psychologists have observed that in conversion, a person enters an exceptional state of intense spiritual and emotional moment. That ecstatic moment overcomes a person suddenly and without a normal participation. It happens due to a human being's excessive concentration on objects related to one's spiritual life and the longing for the soul to be unified with God. We need more research on a total concentration in these internal experiences. Insight into the total disintegration or a total integration, the sense of separating of what is physical form from the mental as an expression of the presence of God.

When scientists analyze specific phenomena of a Christian religious experience in order to understand their origin, course, and meaning in human spiritual life. God manages the natural rights of creation in a free manner. Seekers desire a personal relationship with God.

Transformational conversion with its whole strength tears away from sensory activities and rises to the summit of contemplation and the love of living the vision of God. The religious phenomenon is accompanied by elation, joy, renewal, delight, positive emotionalism, exaltation, and engagement. Being outside yourself is the work of the Holy Spirit to take you to the place where God wants you to be. Read I Samuel 10:5-7 and I Samuel 19:19-24. Imagine this scene. There is a dancing group of prophets. The prophets were a community led by Samuel. The people thought they had gone crazy. As Saul met this procession of prophets, the Holy Spirit took control over Saul. His caused Saul to prophesy. With this experience, God prepared Saul for his calling as king.

People who are near to God's presence are being filled with the Holy Spirit. Peter told the crowd they might think they were drunk. Acts 2:13. What does that tell us about the work of the Spirit? The filling of the Holy Spirit can lead us into an ecstatic experience. The filling of the Spirit releases spiritual gifts. And best of all, the filling of the Spirit leads to extraordinary joy.

More than 300 years ago, "Joy to the World," was written by Isaac Watts. It is considered as the most joyous hymns for Christmas. It can be sung anytime with the deep realization of what Christ's birth has meant for humankind. The hymn is a paraphrase of Psalm 98. Watts gave the Psalm a fresh interpretation. It composed it as a New Testament expression of praise for the salvation that began when God became incarnate.

There is glaring disparity between the hope of joyous life expressed in Jesus. Real joy can be found in the scriptures and in examples from many of his followers. People condemn and judge Christians considering Jesus and his healing words. A disciple of Jesus grows in grace and knowledge of Jesus. Read II Peter 3:18.

The joy of salvation includes being a learner, a student, an apprentice, and a practitioner. Joyful disciples do not just profess certain views as their own, but they must apply their understanding of life in the Kingdom of Joy on earth as in heaven. Congregations come to the table with so many differing agendas. Leaders get a cross purposes with each other because each wants their own way. If we are passionate about knowing God, we will not have any trouble ending up on the same page. The church exists not to meet personal needs, but to reach outwardly to those who do not know God.

In some of our "once saved, always saved" culture, those who have made a profession of faith and are baptized think that they are Christians forever, yet these church members never become disciples. A search through the Bible reveals that the word "disciple" is used 269 times in the New Testament. The word "Christian" is used only three times.

I have noticed that television shows such as "Who Wants to Be a Millionaire?" and "Jeopardy" contestants always miss even the simple questions about the Bible. I have noticed that in all my years of speaking on campus sites that Jesus is dismissed from brilliance or intellectual or things to know. In my 20 years as volunteer campus minister for Southeast Community College in Lincoln, Nebraska, most students shared their anxiety, guilt, and fear in areas such as vocational guidance, choosing a job, a possible spouse, most aimed at more pleasure and pride. Twice a year, I took students for a retreat into solitude and silence. Students are busy people. They take classes, hold down a job, and as older parents or late bloomers, care for others. We sought to help them pray for these areas and people with whom they interact with each day. We often discussed the letter to the Philippians centering our focus on joy and what joy can mean. Campus ministry is a difficult place for evangelism. When joy wells up in the life of a student, we have shared joy that will be multiplied throughout life. Preaching salvation in revivals and as a pastor of local congregations, I have noted and saved by photo, journal, and testimony of 255,881 converts during my 69 years of preaching. Like many other evangelistic preachers, I saw 371,810 make decisions for Christ such as rededications, calls to ministry, guidance in every struggle imaginable. For more than 46 years, God has led me to preach at least one sermon each day. My total attendance is now more than 55 million. Many were the same people when I preach often as a pastor or in other groups that I speak to each week. My largest attendance was a rally in Central Park in New York with more than 120,000. I have spoken to just one other person on some occasions. God has called me to use my gifts to write books and articles, to do pastoral psychotherapy, use radio and television, create newsletters, and with God, experience God's divine pleasure.

A faithful walk with God in discipleship nurtures our joy with Christ. Three actions stand out in my own living out the joy of my salvation. I want to thank someone every day. Is there one person in your life who lives in authentic joy? Write a note and thank that person for her or his example.

I want to grow with joy. I am grateful for those who have enabled the development as a maturing Christian. None of them are famous or rich. For me it's my parents, my schoolteachers, my mail person, my faithful physician, the nurses, my supportive bosses, the garbage people, and those who mow my lawn, or just give me something as a gesture of love. When joy wells up, we want to share it. When God shows up and does something spectacular, we simply cannot remain silent. An answered prayer is divine sunshine bursting through the clouds. Our souls are overjoyed with "the joy of the Lord."

At the beginning of my last service following a pastoral journey of ten years, more than 100 children walked from the back of the church building to the front carrying palm leaves. Children are recipients of the joy as their minds are not misshapen. Their inner ability of perception has not been depleted. Journaling my gratitude and joy times is a pleasing way to record my life. The days of my life can be found in the words written in my journal. Keeping scrapbooks and photographs from my world travels and family activities cause me to bring out those joy videos that are still recorded deep in me. Love is forever.

The church must break fresh ground in its thinking and in is doing. The Spirit will help in the imagination for new ministries that are bold, relevant, pertinent, and effective in fulfilling the vision of God. The congregations must begin to dream dreams worthy of the kingdom.

The church must follow Jesus and nobody else. We realize that if the believers have made the efforts and paid the price, we may go into places we might never have chosen to go in our own volition. When "the joy of the Lord" wells up, we cannot be silent. With God, we are living in the kingdom of heaven on earth, which is the reason Jesus gave its citizens the Great Commission so that abundance life could happen.

In his Great Commission, Jesus instructed his followers to go forth into the world and make disciples Those early Christians' task meant not simply proclaiming, but an effective conversion. The Great Commission would not be published as Christ intended until it was received or attended to by those hearing it. Only when the effective relationship between the gospel and the heater is accomplished may the proclamation be fully communicated. **PASSIONATE Joy** Believers are passionate about what God is passionate about. God is not passionate about some things that we get extremely passionate about. Things like what color to paint the new bathroom, keeping children from getting fingerprints on the walls of the fellowship hall, the use of pews or chairs in the sanctuary, our styles of music, the contents of the church constitution and bylaws, or who will be permitted to use the new basketball gymnasium. God is passionate about the salvation of people. God is passionate about having intimacy with people. Passion is clearly visible in the life, death, and resurrection of Jesus. God is passionate about people who do not know why Jesus came to earth. Read John 3:16. We need to reevaluate where passions lie.

Passionate chronicles of the kingdom journey are beyond the formulas and concepts of contemporary expressions of Christianity. With the passionate joy of the Lord the Spirit of Joy church will become less passionate about those things that distract us from fulfilling the mission God requires from us. Leo Tolstoy wrote, "Joy can only be real if people look upon their life as a service and have a definite object in life outside themselves and their personal happiness. "All our stories are unique, but we all have a story. Our stories are the way to encourage one another in the evangelistic effort of seeing the kingdom of God on earth look like the kingdom that is in heaven. The more stories we share, the more understanding we have about what God is doing around the world. Everybody in the Body of Christ has a story. We need to hear it if the cultural congregations are to be changed.

Conversion is such a vital topic. Researchers in the field of psychology reveal the significant psychological contributions to the study of religious conversion. In the past decade, there has been a broadening of the contemporary and growing literature concerning conversion.

Psychological research helps us understand the joy of salvation. The American Psychological Association defines joy as "a feeling of extreme gladness, delight, or exaltation of the spirit arising from a sense of well-being or satisfaction." APA research discovered that joy activates the parasympathetic nervous system. This promotes feelings of calm and peacefulness. We see this in those who are doing the Great Commission such as Mother Teresa. Her life was surrounded by suffering, pain, and death, yet she was joyful. Joy is found in unlikely places. Joy needs an environment that promotes joy. It is much easier to notice negative things and let the possibilities for joy slip by. Simply pausing to appreciate the atmosphere can enable one to better cultivate joy. Scientific studies find that telling others about your joy has incredible benefits.

Look for the stories of the conversion of believers to cultivate the joy. The joy of the Lord can be found in surprising places.

Two major areas have been recognized. One is that people experience a variety of types of spiritual changes beyond the initial conversion. Secondly, conversion occurs not only inside a religious setting, but in those unexpected times and places.

Researching shows the focus was and often is about dramatic religious conversions transformed by an emotion process. This happens most of the time during adolescence. This growing awareness of spiritual and religious diversity has led to question of our models of conversion. Psychologists and sociologists defined conversion as a "radical transformation of the self." One study suggested that conversion involves "a person divided and consciously inferior, wrong, and unhappy, becomes superior, right, and happy." (L. R. Rambo, *Understanding Religious Conversion*, pp. 34-35)

Rambo's research brought an insight that conversion involves a radical result of a change in values, identity, concerns, and actions. The converted go from disinterest to intimacy with the sacred. This also can indicate a quest beyond religious tradition by searching for fresh new meanings. His model of conversion emphasized spiritual seeking new meanings within a contemporary paradigm. (L. R. Rambo, *Ibid.*, pp. 23-28.

Another study likened conversion to an infatuation involving emotional turmoil. Conversion is like falling in love. The focus was on the emotional and relational dynamics of religious conversion. Carol Ullman noted conversion is the pursuit

of a haven of salvation in relationship to a parental figure or love object. She said many conversions show emotional distress before conversion. Her sample quest shows another motivation is a quest for existential meaning. Spiritual behaviors represent attempts of dwell within the safety and security of God's love. (Carol Ullman, *The Transformed Self: The Psychology of Religious Conversion*, pp. 2-12.

Each of the above psychological models employ cognitive psychology. Also, advances in neurobiology contribute to these models of conversion. Sociocultural and context outside a person and intrapsychic factors enable us to understand the process of conversion. (R.F. Paloutzian, *Handbook of the Psychology of Religion and Spirituality*, pp. 331-377)

His research shows conversion is shaped by prior experience, His is oriented toward creativity and new meaning. He sees conversion as non-linear and inclusive of dark nights of the soul bringing spiritual ambiguity and struggle. Paloutzian stated that conversion is an on-going process of attempting to balance conversion with struggles and discontinuities as catalysts for change. His model integrated psychology with the spiritual tradition of contemplative Christian spirituality. (Palutzian, *Ibid.*, pp. 388-402)

Each study involved a thorough review of the literature to date to investigate the impact of conversion on human personality. This recent research suggests that conversions do not change basic personality. They found that the chief effects of personality changes consisted in an increase of positive emotion such as joy.

Positive effects appeared to have been sustained for 20 or more years.

The entire history of inquiry into conversion attests to profound shifts in the way one perceives God. The theme of redemption fills one's stories of the negative into a positive attitude that leads to caring for others. These redemptive identities are influenced by religious traditions. Secular versions of redemptive narratives are sources of idealization like those in Christian conversion.

Current research finds that emotional concerns, motivations and behaviors not only changing as a result of conversions, but we find them in the impetus behind conversions.

An emerging interest in the field of psychology of religion has directed scholars' attention. The complex and reciprocal relationship between the cultural worldview and fresh modern insights hold the key to understanding conversion.

One advance in research is the growing number of empirical studies that explicitly tested theoretical models of conversion. My reading in the literature demonstrated six areas in my own understanding and teaching within my vision of the Great Commission. These are a zealous dedication, openness to uncertainty, redemptive love, dysphoric need, life crises, and experiential learning. The only difference between the traditional conversion and a gradual religious change was in levels of life transformation. The studies suggest future work on spiritual conversion would benefit from the investigation of nonlinear effects as well as inclusion of measures and methods that continue the truth of this important issue.

Like many areas in the sociological and psychological research, one limitation is that samples are predominantly from overrepresentation of American and European samples and research contexts. The distinctions between conversion and salvation suggest theological nuances and the need for more interdisciplinary collaboration between social scientists and religious scholars.

Integration could be enhanced as social scientists collaborate with religious scholars to accurately interpret indigenous understandings. For my Psy.D. dissertation at Oxford University, I wrote "The Integration of Joy in Clinical Family Counseling."

"Joy is a decision, a really brave one, about how you are going to respond to life." -- Wess Stafford

Chapter Three
JOY IN THE KINGDOM

In our class in journalistic photography, the instructor often reminded us, a picture is worth a thousand words. Images are powerful. The risk in the use of images. The possibility that the significance of the imagery may not be clear. In Acts 2:30, we consider tongues of fire to describe the image of the Holy Spirit. When the day of Pentecost arrived, the followers of Jesus were together in one place. Suddenly there came a sound like a rushing wind, and the house was filled. Tongues like *"feu de joie"* or "the fire of joy" rested on each one. Acts 2:1-3. Fire represents the presence of eternal God.

Fire is a symbol of sanctification. The meaning of sanctification is "the process by which an entity is brought in relationship with or attains the likeness of the holy. (D.R.W. Wood and Marshall I. Howard, *New Bible Dictionary*, p. 1058) In Psalm 66:10, we read of God refining us in fire as silver purging away sin. The image of fire burns into us an increased sense of urgency to share the gospel with others.

Fire is contagious and difficult to contain. When the fire of the Spirit consumes us, it would be impossible to keep the gospel withing ourselves. God needs people who are filled with anointing holy fire. It is God's command that we spread the Word of God like wildfire in this world that is starved for love and the fire of joy.

The flickering of a flame brings thoughts of desire and passion. Fires leap, dance, and spread with abandon. The best way to describe two lovers is remarking about their "fiery passion." The expression, "light my fire," means someone inspired passion with somebody's soul. The image of fire was used in "Romeo and Juliet" to symbolize the passion two young people feel for each other.

When a fire rages in a forest, the old growth in the forest burns away to allow space for a new forest to emerge from beneath like a rebirth and a resurrection.

Joy in the kingdom of God comes by God's grace. In expressing my view of evangelism or anything else, I guide people to soak up the Bible. Read I John 3:16-18; Romans 14:17-18; I Corinthians 12:24-37.

Scripture clearly says that God does not desire to keep joy in heaven, but to fill us with this overflowing joy. Joy comes from the Holy Spirit within us. In intimacy with God, we know abundant times of joy. We shall rejoice in God above all else. When we lean on God as the source of a sure foundation. When our emotions change with the tides in the world, joy will come and go like waves. To experience God's challenge, we must trust in God's dreams. We sing together, "This is the day that the Lord has made. Let us rejoice and be glad in it. Psalm 118:24. Each day of our lives on earth was created by God. We have joy in our earthly trials when we trust God. Read James 1:2-4. James is saying that unceasing joy comes from living with God rather than with allegiance to the world. Spending quality time in God's presence and allowing the Spirit to bear fruit inside is the unshakable foundation of God's love. In your secret place, meditate on God's desire to fill you with abounding joy. Read John 15:11, Romans 14:17, Galatians 5:22.

Reflect on your own life journey. Where are you not experiencing joy? What can take away joy? In every area of life practice submission. Receive the joy of Jesus. Allow God to reveal God's heart for every situation. **The Redemptive Fellowship of the Church** the Christian Church has the ability, gifts, and graces to demonstrate the love of God through human relationships. In a Spirit of Joy Church, a believer can discover tangible expressions of the grace that endows life. The body of Christ is a partnership where seekers share a common devotion to Christ. Living in the kingdom of God means to connect inner living with outer conduct with the transforming power of the Spirit. Christians are taught to see themselves to be what God envisions life to be.

In these my later years, I have investigated a mirror and I see a joyful man staring back. Occasionally, I wonder why I feel so much joy. When my brother David died, I felt a mixture of sadness and joy. Charles Dickens wrote, "The pain of parting is nothing to the joy of meeting again."

The evidence that this is happening between each disciple is that the same relationship that Christ had with his disciples is found within the church. When unbelievers observe clear and humble communications between Christians in the church, they see evidence of the presence of God. If they do not see this, the gospel is tightly bound. The redemptive fellowship of the church gives a purpose for living.

If God's love is incarnate in the fellowship of the church, others will be attracted to this image. This is evangelism incarnate in the redemptive conversion process. Within the kingdom of God on earth we ae called to care for the least of these. Some are vulnerable to Covid-19. These include the elderly, people with weak immune systems, the poor, the unemployed. This causes us to see the Great Commission to require extra and extraordinary ministries.

Christians are called to feed the hungry and to clothe and house the homeless. During the current pandemic, believers have opportunities to act on Jesus' imperative. The pandemic causes some to devalue human life. Those who are most vulnerable are pitted against the less vulnerable and those with chances for survival. "Lest of these" are left behind. These do not line up with Christian teachings or vital actions. The elderly become no longer valued for their life experiences and wisdom. There are now levels of human value. A kingdom response requires admitting our failure as a nation to provide the medical resources, so that those who need medical care can get it.

The Word "kingdom" appears 157 times in the New Testament. The phrase "kingdom of God" occurs 53 times in the gospels and 14 times outside the four gospels. From a statistical view, the theme of the kingdom is a major concern for the synoptics—Matthew, Mark, and Luke—but less concern in the rest of the Scriptures. Read Matthew 4:17, Mark 1:14-15, and Luke 4:16-21. In the beginning of the public ministry of Jesus, I have compared Matthew, Mark, and Luke in the above verses. The preaching on the kingdom continued through his three-year ministry. Christian disciples must understand his message about the kingdom of God. The phrase "the kingdom of God" is not used in the Old Testament. Jesus said, "The time is fulfilled, and the kingdom of God is at hand." Mark 1:15. There are some Old Testament passages that describe God's realm. Read I Chronicles 29:31, Psalm 103:19, Psalm 145:10-13, Daniel 4:34, and Daniel 6:26. Both Isaiah 40 and Isaiah 52 connect the hope of God's coming kingdom to the gospel. Read Isaiah 52:7-10. This hope appears to be a single event which will be a mighty demonstration of God's power which would sweep away the evil kingdoms where humans rule and the earth would be filled with righteousness. In one sense of understanding the New and Old Testaments is that God has always reigned over creation with authority. In Daniel 2:40, 44-45, the writer prophesies the coming kingdom of God.

The ministry of the early church and that of Paul confirms that Jesus did establish the kingdom of heaven on earth. Read Acts 8:5-7,12, 19:8-10, 28:23 30-31. According to Acts, to preach the kingdom of God was to preach about Jesus. Kingdom service means loving one another. This brings wells of joy in our living and in the church. In my book, *Spirit of Joy Church*, I describe congregations as the Spirit of Guilt Church, the Spirit of Anger Church, the Spirit of Anxiety Church, the Spirit of Fear Church, and finally the Spirit of Joy Church. When our church becomes a Spirit of Joy Church, joy wells up in our souls and in the hearts of the recipients.

Kingdom people are free to operate with minimum restraint and without having their passions dampened by endless permission-seeking steps in complex structures. We must remove as many obstacles as possible. A guided autonomy is one way of expression the work of the kingdom. Too many ministers and ministries feel abandoned. They feel encouragement and support. They are not challenged nor are they limited.

The apostle Paul found joy in those who God placed in his care. We rejoice for those things we find in each other. Read II Corinthians 6:3-10; 7:13.

We can read verses on the kingdom of God in Matthew, Mark, and Luke. The words "kingdom of heaven" appears in Matthew only. There we read it32 times.

In gatherings of others we pray for the kingdom to come. We need to preach and teach about the kingdom. We seek to be agents of forgiveness. We pray for healing the sick. Read James 5:16. God has ultimate control over sickness. See Deuteronomy 32:39.

We work together to advance the kingdom. We are willing to suffer for the kingdom. Scripture teach that sickness, death, and all human suffering were introduced into the world as a result of humankind's fall into sin. Read Genesis3 and Romans 8. Prayers include medical means as needed. See I Timothy 5:23.

The ministry of healing in churches is not an end, but a sign of Christ's spiritual power. As we envision the Great Commission including God placing a hand for healing so humans might be led to see that Jesus is Lord. The ministry of healing, along with the ministry of the Word and ministries of mercy, are to be included for envisioning the strategy for both local and world evangelism until the kingdom is fully realized.

The world-wide pandemic and our greedy political environment yield not only evil, but loss of hope. In the presence of the 21st Century world, it results in giving up on the goodness of God and life itself. Today's quest for joy with superficial pleasures include seizing what a person can get for one's self. At the present time in history, the Christian concept of the coming of the kingdom of God affirms that this is still God's world. I believe that we will know and see those we have loved on earth. The ties of love will be preserved. We now pray "thy kingdom come," in expectation and anticipation that we must work for the kingdom now. The vision of the kingdom was summed up by Paul as he wrote that the kingdom consists of "righteousness and peace and joy in the Holy Spirit. "The goals of the kingdom involve our personal living and a new society in the future for which we give obedient service and prayer.

All is well. We can be confident that we will live forever despite the dissolution of the body or a final cataclysm that may destroy the earth. Wherever we exist in the world, God has given us a network of social relationships that are precious to us. Psalm 68:6 says, "God sets the solitary in families." The family is blood kin, as well as our neighbors, and the entire human family. Sadly, these relationships can become dysfunctional, but at their best bring joy. God is love. Love is forever. Love cannot be ended forever by the death of the body. During the intervening years, we will miss the life and love of those so precious to us.

In our final years when our bodily strength diminishes, with joy, we can live zestfully and do what we still have the power to do.

Joy and gratitude are to be our response to spiritual and physical well-being in this earthly journey and in the next place. Remember that Luke 16:19-26teaches that the healthy, rich man went to hell. The poor man full of sores went to heaven.

The kingdom of joy is both present and future is the theme of the description of eternal life presented in the gospel of John. John tells us that we enter eternal life by becoming a believer in Christ. This includes our mind and our commitment. Believing or as John said is being born anew. See John 3:3,5. We have eternal life after death as is so eloquently written in John 14:1-3.

"Thy kingdom come" is for now as well as the future. Our human life journey with its difficulty, suffering, and aimlessness has a purpose. The soul is so valuable in the kingdom that God's plan is to give it eternal life.

The journey toward a better world, fulfills the vision of the kingdom. Life is a rugged journey. And life beyond death will be filled with joy. Freedom from the body we needed on earth will bring joy for the aged or terminally ill when life's road ends. The fellowship with God's intimate love will be preserved in the kingdom of joy. Psalm 71:23 refers to singing. "My lips will shout for joy, when I sing praises to you; my soul also, which you have redeemed." Joy is such a powerful emotion. God created music so we could express joy.

Maintaining the Joy Of Salvation

When that love of God first touched us, a deep joy that we had never known filled us. God wants us to continue to rejoice in God's gift of salvation. In understanding of evangelism and conversion, the normal experience of every believer. Read I Peter 1:8. As we seek to find fresh ways of doing evangelism, one evidence is overflowing with unspeakable joy.

Sin causes us to lose the joy of salvation. After a conversion experience, humans still sin, fail and disobey God. After we choose to sin, we know that something is wrong. See Isaiah 59:2. We now need a new point of focus. The Holy Spirit restores the joy as Jesus' life overcomes the fracture of desire in the image of an invisible God. Sitting still and looking at an image of Christ and God's saving work leads me into an intimate communion with God.

Grieving the Holy Spirit causes us to lose the joy. In Romans 8:9, Paul tells us that "the Spirit of God dwells in you." Jesus said the kingdom of God is within us. There is joy in heaven when we decide on living a new life. To restore joy, we need to confess sin quickly. Whenever our conscience makes us aware that we have sinned ignites confession time. Read I John 1:9. Read God's Word each day. Eating physical food brings pleasure. Eating the scriptures brings inner satisfaction. In my book, *The Joy of Prayer: The Way to Intimacy with God*, I write about prayer as the key to the kingdom joy. By this fellowship of talking and mostly listening to God, joy moves in lightly like a faint breeze. Joy washes in like a sudden wave. As we share that joy, we keep overflowing joy. **Finding the Joy of God's Kingdom** "The kingdom of God is . . . joy in the Holy Spirit." Romans 14:17. My family and family congregation sing "Joy to the World." The Church Fathers seize the opportunity to cover the pagan feasts of the sun's conquering winter solstice with Christmas. The deeper joy of anticipating the coming Messiah makes walking by faith and not by sight possible. II Corinthians 5:7. The Sermon on the Mount is more than just ethical teaching. God's guidance calls for renewed repentance preceded by conversion. Mercy and forgiveness bring on the kingdom filled with the joy of new life. (Joachim Jeremias, *Sermon on the Mount*, pp. 12-23)

The Sermon on the Mount is not an interim ethic. It is an exciting glimpse into the reality of the kingdom of heaven. C. S. Lewis used the analogy of God's revelation being like the transition of a higher, more sophisticated language with an awesome vocabulary into a simpler language. Hat is an effective way to describe the breaking into the human sphere from the divine way. The Word of God is Jesus and his incarnation. The Bible is called the Word of God, the revealed truth that is mediated through humans in the Old and New Testaments. The space-time of the kingdom begins here and now. The kingdom of joy is subsumed into eternity. (C.S. Lewis, *The Weight of Glory and Other Addresses*, p. 27-29)

Today's cultural church has quite a bit of unlearning to do. God sees our acts clearly, allowing for the consequences for free will, but never gives up. Spiritual formation with humility allows us to acknowledge sin within, and the possibility of restoring intimacy with God which brings joy. Without this possibility for joy, why would we look beyond ourselves? The Sermon on the Mount gives snapshots of heaven. The kingdom is a house built on a rock, being the salt of the earth, being cared for like the lilies of the field, and bring peace and reconciliation instead of hate and strife.

Zacchaeus climbed a sycamore tree to see Jesus. He was a short man, a chief tax collector for the Roman government. Jesus stopped as he walked through crowds of people in Jericho. "Zacchaeus! Hurry and come down because I am going home with you today."

He had grown up hating his fellow citizens because he was treated so poorly. After Jesus shared with him, he was healed of his hate and the need to get even. Zacchaeus was converted that day. He told Jesus he was going to give half of all he possessed to the poor. Think about your own life journey. Imagine Jesus coming into your life as he did with this wealthy tax collector. Part of the transformation might now include giving half away. That would include your home, your cars, your clothing, your savings accounts, your books, your silverware, your furniture, your paintings, your golf clubs, your retirement account. Think what that mean in the poor in Jericho that day. Those people, like many in our day, lived at the edge of starvation. What if we responded to the presence of Jesus the way done by a collector of taxes? He started leaning on God, sharing all his struggles. Zacchaeus no longer felt scared, anxious, overwhelmed, or inferior because of his short statue. Without Jesus' guidance, we will go back to our selfish ways, and focus on the wrong things. We are comforted by God's joy. Psalm 94:19, KJV. What we need to remember is that there is a Spirit who reminds us to continue to think effective thoughts. Our thoughts become our lives. Know that we might not receive what we desire as we envisioned it. Psalm 37:4.

Have we thought about doing what Zacchaeus felt he wanted to do? What if your conversion to Christ included the words, "I love what Jesus has done to give a new life? I am going to share half of what I own with people who need what I am able to give." (John Killinger, *The Zacchaeus Solution: A Novel*, pp. 57-59

Conversion brings a new set of habits. James writes, "Show me your faith without deeds, and I will show you my faith by my deeds. James 2:18. Often we observe faith being exhibited in action. Action shapes faith. Transfer that idea to faith. Faith is not an act, a single choice, or even a belief system. Faith is a habit.

Most Americans hold the view that getting married, building a career, buying a house, and raising a family are desirable milestones. These are American societal habits. Personal habits shape our values. The church often overlooks the habit part of discipleship.

In my church leadership, I have insisted on "quiet time" as essential to nourishing faith. Some mainline and other church groups have left it by the wayside. Evangelism is not concerned with church growth, but with living in the kingdom of joy. If our only habits are going to church and attending meetings, that will not connect us into the lives of unbelievers nor invite their curiosity about the faith journey.

Christians need habits that do not just deplete our energy and burn us out, but those that re-energize us, replenishing reserves and connecting us to deep joy with Jesus.

If you bless two people each week, you will become a generous person. If you eat with others, you will develop hospitality. If you listen to the Spirit, you will become a Spirit-led person. In the process, you are learning Christ, and will become more like Jesus.

People being habitually loved can relive burdens, help them breath, lift their sad moods, alleviate their distress. I enjoy using Gary Chapman's love language books in family life conferences. Briefly he gives five habits: Words of affirmation, acts of kindness, giving gifts, touch, and helps.

My retirement congregation is called the Spirit of Joy Christian Church. The habit of eating together has created a community during the Covid-19 pandemic as we wear a mask and keep distance.

Christian faith witnesses to the joy in sharing food with others. It is difficult to delight when one cannot share. Learning to share deeply with others brings a mindfulness. Church groups can share time-honored eating as joy in community. Eating in communion leads to satisfying relationships with other people, with ourselves, and with God. Saying grace at meals promotes humility and reminds us of injustices that keep others hungry. Sharing food is to share having food to share. When my wife was gone on one of her trips with Diane Bish, I was home alone with lots of food. On a cold day in Nebraska, I went downtown to share my joy and to give food to people who were staying overnight in dumpsters. We have a deep need to share. We share joy in sharing. We have a food bank in our town in Cass County, Nebraska. God created us with inner instincts to seek not only our well-being, but that of others. The promise is there is enough for all creatures. Using my and John Killinger's favorite word for joy, we are capable of *jouissance*, the French word for food and pleasure. Keep aware of your joy life videos, the times when the hospitality and food clicks and everyone feels secure and relaxed.

In my mind's eye, I can hear my daughter Linda saying "God is great. God is good. Let us thank God for our food. Amen." I love the prayers that are formulated on the spot. Saying grace is important. If it does little else, it preserves a form of asking God's blessing. People share a common humanity. The differences between rich and poor, male and female, young and old, black and white and brown and yellow are small in the joy of relating. Practicing hospitality is a matter of love. Being in life together with God and the world is the kingdom of God. In breaking bread together, we experience God's energy.

When discussing the early Christians, historians noted, "Look, these people love each other." The early church fathers when sharing their joy of salvation in the Greco-Roman world, they spoke of how Christian believers loved others as themselves. This marked them as being followers of Jesus. Love carried them through severe persecution.

Early Christian communities attempted to feed the poor, host travelers, visit the imprisoned, invite orphans and widows to join them at mealtime. Dr. Hugh Wamble, the beloved professor of church history at Midwestern Theological Seminary in Kansas City, often quoted the *Didache*, a second century text, that instructed Jesus' followers to help visiting travelers. Wamble would often cite the fourth century preacher John Chrysostom to welcome strangers as guests. When people come into our community, we are to thank God for them, and thank God for what God will do for them while they are with us.

During one of our annual convocations for learning and love feasting at a conference center in Nebraska, a little note was shared. A participant wrote: "How can I tell you all that is deep in my soul as I leave this place? I came empty and despairing. Leaving no, I continue to suffer pain, but now in joy, I am strengthened for healing. I was hungry and you feed me, a stranger and you took me in, and my life will never be the same."

The process of preparing bread and wine for a Holy Communion is done privately by one or two people. Some may be lay deacons. How could a church prepare communion that reflects the fact that it is the whole congregation that needs to prepare for communion in gathered worship?

Conversion flowers from communion. Jesus ate at the home of the tax collector Zacchaeus. Jesus' communion meal with him led to repentance and conversion.

I have a habit of journaling. For many years I have kept a journal. It reminds me of what happened, when, and with whom. I have long forgotten some joy times, but often I can find them in one of my journals. With my habit of journaling I list various ways that I have alerted others to God, identifying my calling as Minister of Joy to the World. I alert others to my joy both by talking about them (witness) and demonstrating them (action).

May God consecrate our congregations for your purposes. May the Lord lead to the discovery of peace, awe, wonder, and joy that comes from being a part of the kingdom of joy. The kingdom goal is in the presence of Christ to reach outward to a hurting and lost world.

Those hurting souls are difficult to love. Each is unique and it is difficult to "love your neighbor as you love yourself." It is a hard task to love impossible people. They bother us because they do not know or live by our cultural context. We just hate the negative qualities they bring out in us. Jesus tells us to "love our enemies, bless them that curse you, do good to them that hate you, and pray for them which despitefully use you, and persecute you. "Matthew 5:44, KJV. We try to forget the reality that they exist. God's joy creates compassion for millions who missed the point of their existence. Compassion adds to a Christian's inner bliss. It never diminishes it. Joy is what humans are seeking. This bliss is not a side issue. The more we feel inner joy, the more she longs to share it. Joy is what awakens compassion. Compassionate love emanates from God. It comes with the Spirit so that joy becomes the channel through which the love of God flows out into the world.

Producing a beautiful diamond requires cutting the stone along its natural cleavage. The cut must not be random. Conversion brings out the beauty in human nature. The redeemed sense a newfound unexpected door to joy.

Scripture has much to say about finding joy in the act of sharing it. Encourage one another. I Thessalonians 5:11. Greet one another. Romans 16:16. Regard one another as most important. Philippians 2:4. Pray for one another. James 5:16. Admonish one another. Colossians 3:16. Serve one another. Galatians 5:13. Forgive one another. Ephesians 4:32. Accept one another. Romans15:7. Love one another. I John 3:11. The Bible and research confirms doing good does good for the doer. The lonely planet earth lacks love and kindness. Christians cannot solve every problem, but we can bring smiles to a few faces. As we brighten the corners of the world, a quiet revolution of joy might break out.

"When our words are filled with wisdom, they produce joy." –Albert Schweitzer

Chapter Four
The Biblical Concept of Conversion

Conversion is necessary for aligning our lives with the kingdom of God. In the Bible, conversion is often pictured in its abrupt transformational form. Spiritual conversion brings renewed understanding of personal and public ethics. Salvation involves the individual and the social, the personal holy living and justice.

Conversion is not only about our escape from judgement in the afterlife, but it is about obeying the commands, principles, and priorities of the kingdom of God. The actions to escape such horror is not through an intellectual assent to a long list of doctrines, or repeating words from a penitential prayer, or abstaining from harmful social practices. It does mean following Jesus each day, motivated by love, demonstrating what it is to live freely and joyfully as people of God. Conversion involves the whole person. Being converted is to believe, to have a new sense of what is good and evil, and to shun former pleasures as now binging wasteful and toxic. Being transformed into new life, one finds beauty where nothing worthwhile was found. The Bible sums up the central command of Jesus to love each other. John 13:34-35. God continues to work inside us to stretch boundaries, enabling us to love those who are differing from us. Jesus even taught us to love our enemies. Read Hebrews 13:1-3.

Conversion is an encounter with the love and grace of God in Christ. The process continues in our discovery of joy in acting in love with one another. It extends and gathers strength as we discern and pursue opportunities to share grace, mercy, and peace with our neighbors. Small acts of countercultural love with the Spirit as strength will shake strongholds and changes as we love next door or those living far away.

The Kingdom of God is nearer to us than we often think. Every day, we are called by the voice of God to follow Jesus into the kingdom. Crossing over through conversion into his kingdom requires faith and dependence on the mercy and grace of God. Praying in intimacy with God for the grace and mercy, we can empty ourselves of worldly things and enter the kingdom.

Thomas Merton, the articulate monk who died in 1969, said of his conversion, "A door opened in the center of my being. I fell through it into immense depths. This is accessible to all of us all eternity sems to have become mine in this placid and breathless contact."

The Christian paradox is that we live in this world with our souls burning for the next world. The Bible teaches us that clearly the world has fallen, redeemed, and awaiting re-creation. The kingdom of God is already and not yet. Joy flows from a deeply rooted conviction that not only does God cause all things to work together for the good of those who love the Lord. Joy is restored as we live in God's kingdom of joy. Psalm 51:12. Joy is found in delighting in God's Word. Psalm 97:11. The Bible is an inheritance from the Lord. It is better than diamonds, gold, or rubies. And it has been passed down to us. Joy results as we speak with wisdom. Proverbs 15:23. The desire of God is that we speak life-giving words to those in our circle of influence. Joy is found in God's presence. Psalm 16:11. The Bible tells us that we make a determined effort to spend intimate hours with God. Joy is a result of our prayers. John 16:24. Making special times to pray makes room for more joy. It is "the joy of the Lord" that is produced by the Holy Spirit. Galatians 5:22.

Trust these biblical concepts for God loves us more than we can imagine. God has more power than we can comprehend. When I think of the people God has placed in my earthly journey in the kingdom, I leap in joy.

The accounts of conversion in the Scriptures give the most believable basis to re-evaluate and define conversion. First, I shall evaluate the biblical terms for conversion in the Old and New Testaments. The biblical concepts ensure that conversion and evangelism practices are congruent with teaching of the Word.

The Hebrew Scriptures' concept of repentance helps us understand the New Testament understanding about conversion. The Old Testament reveals that God calls Israel and the Gentile nations to repent. As God seeks the salvation of the people of God, they are determined to turn away. Repentance in the Old Testament is a covenant relationship between God and the people. God asks them to turn away from sinful ways. The people need to admit their wrongs and to feel guilt. They are to display emotion. When God calls Israel to repent, it means turning back with their entire personhood, their wills, emotions, and reason. Psalms enable people to feel every emotion, especially the joy.

In Exodus 19:5, we learn that God descends on the sacred mountain at Sinai clothed in fire and smoke. The prophet Isaiah sees the Lord in glory attended by seraphim, literally, "the burning ones." One of the seraphim, in an act symbolizing purification, touches Isaiah's lips with a burning coal from the fire. God then commissions this man of unclean lips to proclaim the Word of God to the people of Judah. Isaiah 6:1-8.

The fire motif as the presence of God is found throughout the Old Testament as well as the New Testament. Fire is a riveting robust symbol which gets holy attention. Fire causes us to reflect on the character of God.

When God sets us on fire, it is a consuming fire of love, which God is eager to share with us with joy.

The New Testament understanding of repentance focuses on three words: *Metamelomai, epistrepho*, and *metanoeo*.

The Greek word *metamelomai* expresses the feeling in repentance for error, debt, and sin. This word appears only twice in the parable of the two sons. The first son says that he will not go but then regrets (changes his mind) his decision and goes anyway. The second son says he will go work in the vineyard, but he fails to do so. He first one did the will of the father. Jesus is talking to the elders and priests. Jesus concluded his message, "Truly I say unto you that the tax collectors and prostitutes will get into the kingdom before you. John came to you in the way of righteousness and you did not believe him, but the tax collectors and prostitutes did believe him; and you, seeing this, did not even feel remorse afterward so as to believe him. Read Matthew 21:31-32. The parable indicates that the verbal agreement between his father and his second son was not sufficient to enter the kingdom of heaven. Repentance has an emotional insight of the feelings as one does wrong, which is expressed externally though actions. The New Testament is a book about disciples, by disciples, and for the disciples of Jesus Christ. New Testament Greek words for conversion are *metaneo* and *epistrepho*. The second word occurs 36 times, meaning different types of turning or changing. This word when Jesus rebukes Peter in Mark 8:33. In 18 times, it means conversion with a negative "turning from sin." The positive means "turning to" God. *Epistropho* shows that conversion involves turning away from sin to turning toward God. *Metaneo* emphasizes "turning from" as Jesus and John the Baptist proclaimed, "Repent, for the kingdom of heaven is at hand." Read Matthew 3:2; 4:17.

In the gospel of Mark 1:15, Jesus says, "The time is fulfilled, and the kingdom of God is at hand; repent and believe in the gospel." Believing puts a Christian into the body of Christ. Believing in Christ is the initial point of conversion. Read John 20:31. In a favorite Bible verse, John 3:16, we see the connection between believing in Jesus and eternal life. "To believe," according to John is to believe that Jesus is the Son of God who brings salvation to humankind.

The Holy Scripture provides many accounts dealing with conversion using distinct Greek words. To conceive conversion, study the New Testament texts that uses stories, metaphors, and imagery to convey aspects of conversion. There is no doubt in the biblical picture of human life, that were meant to be inhabited by God. We are to live by the power beyond ourselves. Human problems cannot all be solved by human means. Human life could not flourish without "immeasurable greatness of God's power for us who believe." Ephesians 1:19. **Conversion in the Gospel of John**

Nicodemus functions as a representative of a type of faith. The phrase "born again" is used in discussions about conversion. Nicodemus is mentioned three times in John 2:23-3:16; 7:50-52; 19:39-42. This account is framed within John's larger concern of the kind of belief that leads to the joy in Jesus' name. Before Nicodemus is introduced, John writes that many had believed in Jesus' name. Most of them held an inadequate faith based on a wrong interpretation of signs and miracles Jesus had performed. Some said that he was "the son of God." John uses the phrase "now there was a man" as he introduces Nicodemus. Nicodemus comes with this inadequate faith. Read John 3:1-16.

Conversion and the Gift of the Holy Spirit

Conversion involves receiving the gift of the Holy Spirit. The Holy Spirit brings the birth from above. "Evangelism" or faith-sharing can get us there, but it is the work of God, not humans, that does the converting. None of us can say, "I saved so many souls." Salvation is a gift from God. The Scriptures make it clear that there is a strong connection between the Holy Spirit and the release of extraordinary joy. Just like wine can make you "woozy" and "tipsy" in a joyful way, so does being converted by the Spirit lads you to feeling positive with a quality of eternity. Read Acts 13:52, Romans 15:13, and I Peter 1:8.

The experience of conversion does not have to be that extreme. The Spirit can release in us a much quieter sense of inner joy. Anticipate being surprised by joy when it happens as you pray in your private life. The more time and space you give to the Holy Spirit, the more God can do. Nobody can force the Holy Spirit. We cannot demand God's gifts. We can only welcome, open, and give the Spirit time and space. We do not have to be ecstatic. Doing the work of Jesus' Great Commission gives us much more to discover in the quest for the sacred moments that lift us above the ordinary in epiphanies that rewire our lives.

Millions of people in the last 100 years are told to say the sinner's prayer and they are declared as converted. The sinner's prayer is not biblical. It is not found in the Bible one time.

There are many versions of this prayer. Most are articulated in one such prayer: "Heavenly Father, I know that I am a sinner and I deserve to go to hell. I believe that Jesus died on the cross for my sins. I do now receive Jesus as my Savior and Lord. I promise to serve you to the best of my ability. Please save me now. "Scripture never quotes this prayer or any variation of it. In recent church history, human beings believe this the way for experiencing conversion.

The sinner's prayer originated in the United States. It was popularized by some evangelists and in the traditional local or community church revival. Scriptures tell us "there is a way that seems right to a man, but the end thereof is the way of death." Proverbs 16:25.

Some justify the sinner's prayer by referring to Acts 2:21 where Peter preaches "whoever calls on the name of the Lord shall be saved." This passage is certainly not teaching that people must say a sinner's prayer for conversion.

An incorporation into the Christian community is the theme in the book of Acts. New converts are immediately invited into the community. Read Acts 2:42-44; 9:16. Paul tells us that believers are joined in the Body of Christ.

In Romans 5-8, Paul contrasts life in Adam with a convert's life in Christ. Conversion is not a new status the Holy Spirit gives. It is an experience of wholeness as we become not a servant to sin and death, but to becoming a servant of Christ. We become "instruments of righteousness." Romans 6:13.

Conversion has ethical implications. It is certainly not the truth that Christians no longer sin. Conversion does mean that sin does not rule in our lives. That comes as a gift in the power of the Holy Spirit to live life in God.

Conversion can be instantaneous or a process. In Acts 2:38-41, Peter preached on God's plan and 3,000 listeners responded in what appears to be instantaneous conversion. Forgiveness of sin and salvation in the Acts account are immediately given. Conversion in the life of Paul is a process of at least three days. Acts 9.

There is no set pattern. In Acts 10:44-47, Cornelius receives the gift from the Holy Spirit before he was baptized. The conversion process is not clear-cut. The experience is sometimes ambiguous, but in the process, people receive assurance and clarity about conversion.

Conversion is received by different people in different ways. It is a grace gift from God. Not every conversion is as drastic as Paul's conversion. Surprised by joy initiated by a mysterious and predictable God describes my conversion and calling as minister of joy to the world.

God acts in all human history. Paul Scherer, my friend John Killinger's professor at Princeton, states, "From start to finish the biblical writers are concerned first and foremost with the mighty saving acts of God. The historian records them, the prophets proclaim them, and the Psalmists celebrate them." (Paul Scherer, The Word God Sent, New York: Harper and Row, 1965, p. 25)

The Old Testament prophets pointed toward the coming day when God would act to make possible the relationship of wholeness between God and creation. Jeremiah looked with joyous anticipation to the time God would make a new covenant. Read Jeremiah 31; 33. Isaiah expected the arrival of the Messiah. He would establish the eternal kingdom. Read Isaiah 9:6-7.

The Bible insists that salvation is God's work. God takes the initiative in self-disclosure and revelation. When Jesus was born, there was a community of people anticipating the arrival of the Messiah. God arranged a heavenly choir to announce this good news to ordinary shepherds. This was the climax of the redemptive plan of God.

Scripture tells how God is moving toward us, seeking us, calling us, and enabling us to live new life. Faith-sharing is God's idea. (Eddie Fox and George Morris, Faith Sharing. Nashville: Discipleship Resources, reprinted edition, 2000, p. 13) **Baptism and Conversion**

A profession of faith in Christ is the requirement for baptism. In the New Testament, the book of Acts records that the Ethiopian eunuch, Cornelius, and the Philippian jailer were baptized by immersion after their confessions of Jesus. Read Acts 8:34-38; 10:22-48; 16:29-34. The baptism requirement distinguished Christian baptism from Jewish circumcision of male children. The Scripture says that we are converted with faith not through birth, but by belief.

When people consider baptism, they have a thin understanding as to why Jesus commanded that we baptize his disciples. Many associates the water with cleansing. Pastors often say when baptizing a newly professing Christian, "I baptize you by the authority of the First Baptist Church and the command of Jesus." Think what the phrase "all authority" means. The authority of Jesus forms the foundation of all we do. Jesus has all authority to accomplish his will, and his will includes saving a multitude of people through the proclamation of the gospel. The Great Commission is great because it guarantees results. This command guarantees fruit. We should be filled with joy and encouragement in the efforts of the church. We have the authority of Jesus help us to stir up fresh faith for reaching our world now and in the future.

When Jesus addressed the disciples, he was also addressing the church who would follow in the footsteps of the disciples. This is the clear scope of the Great Commission. Jesus called the disciples to proclaim the gospel to all nations until the end of the world. Jesus knew that it would be impossible for his disciples alone to fulfill his vision. Those eleven men received the commission, it is now up to the church to finish it. Christ expects every Christian to be active in preaching and teaching others to obey the commands of Jesus.

In recounts of church history, the church was made the state church of the Roman Empire. When the emperor and his court were baptized, they use sprinkling as a new way for baptism. After the Reformation, Anabaptists and others were killed for what the church called re-baptism. The state church in the United States was the Anglican church. Christians were often drowned by state church officials when they insisted on baptism by immersion.

When I was preaching in Boston, I learned that Baptist and other groups suffered death when they practiced immersion as the symbol of the confession, belief, and commitment which brings salvation. The pastor of the First Baptist Church in Boston showed in the church records that his Boston congregation were the first Baptist church, not the ones in Providence or other places. His church began meeting secretly in a home. The lowering and raising of a person in water is a dramatic illustration of the death of an old life and the beginning of a new life. Read Romans 6:1-11, 10:9.

When I was appointed to six circuit congregations located in the Blue Ridge Mountains in Virginia. There is a huge Baptist influence in southern churches. I had just been ordained as an elder in the United Methodist Church. The members asked me if I would baptize them in the New River by immersion. I asked the district superintendent and he indicated that Methodists could be baptized by any method. About 20 of them were baptized in the river. Some had been baptized as infants. Most churches view baptism as not a saving act. The saving act from God took place in the death and resurrection of Christ Jesus and the believer's acceptance of that new life of joy. The historical record shows the early church carefully taught seekers about the life of Jesus. They examined their own lives before they were baptized. I Peter 3:21 says baptism is a symbol of change and being raised to new life. Those who continue to baptize infants become upset as that same argument the Zwinglian Anabaptists held caused a rift in many churches.

Baptism is a visible bond between all believers. Read I Corinthians 12:13; Galatians 3:28, and Colossians 2:8-3:4. The New Testament church teaches that we are not to refuse to baptize a person because of class, political party, or race. One area that still needs attention is racial reconciliation.

I experienced believer's baptism by immersion at Woodlawn Baptist Church in Bristol, Tennessee. During my spiritual journey, I served in denominations whose culture was baptizing infants. Many now practice confirmation for teens and others to understand what being converted means. In some situations, confirmation is a rite of reception into full membership. Today parents and pastors insist on confirmation. After some often-boring times with a pastor, they are confirmed. And some never show up in a church again.

Many ministers do deep soul searching as they participate in non-immersion baptisms. Whatever the means of baptism, a believer becomes a part of the gathered community, the body of Christ, where people share a common devotion to Jesus. (Samuel Southard, *Pastoral Evangelism*, pp. 72-75) Through the New Testament we wonder how the so enthusiastic spiritually young believers committed to the faith of Jesus with this new quality of life. Their spiritual formation was established in tough conditions. Paul, Silvanus, and Timothy demonstrated that response to the gospel was the key to how to grow spiritually and be devoted followers as the disciples of Christ. Read Titus 2:11-15, Philippians 2:12-13, I Timothy 4:7-8, and I Corinthians 9:24-27 as you take time to reflect and journal some thoughts. The opposite of discipline is neglect. We might consider that a life of instant gratification becomes the wrath of God. God is love shown by God's actions. We are called for endurance and discipline because this is the long road to life. Read Hebrews 12:3-11. Sin is the extra weight that keeps us from running God's race. God's guidance keeps us from running off course.

Paul's ministry to the Thessalonians exemplifies a more effective approach to making disciples by incorporating evangelism into discipleship in a relational setting. Their method built on the natural development of interpersonal relationships essential for spiritual growth. Read I Thessalonians 1:1-4:12.

These scriptures prove that the bearing of good news outward was no longer understood to be one activity of the church, but the activity of God in which Believers are participants because God loves people, not because the church needs to do it. Churches in mission are not sent overseas or to an event. Evangelism is integral to the life of the church. Professional mission boards do not replace the local church. It is the nature of the church wherever it has located.

In mainline churches, evangelism and conversion discussions focus on the influx of the immigrant population. Faith for them is a public affair. New church plants have included a multitude of humanity moving into the United States. These new churches make up the essence of growth as to the total churches and statistical success bring hope for the future.

In Martha Grace Reeses's book, *Unbinding the Gospel*, funded by extensive research of a Duke University Divinity School study, has a chapter on "If You Don't Like Statistics, Skip This Chapter." She writes, "We need to envision the new world within which we are doing evangelism. We need to know our context before we can act effectively." (Martha Reese, *Unbinding the Gospel: Real Life Evangelism*. St. Louis: Chalice Press, 2007, pp. 23-37)

In percentage terms, in the year 2000 there were only half as many mainline Protestants as there were 40 years before. (*Ibid.*, p. 25) She writes about the churches of the 1960s when pews were full. Reese's book is one of the better volumes created by the mainline writers.

I was so moved by a participant in a Visionquest who wrote, "You have opened my eyes and I now can see. Your explanation of the proclamation of the kingdom though simple yet every word so full of a depth of meaning. I do not understand why I could not grasp this for so many years. I know that when the student is ready a teacher appears. Pray for me that I will always remain teachable. "With Christ speaking through me and my own experience of conversion, I know it is not easy. When Jesus sent out his disciples, he said that they went out "as sheep in the midst of wolves."

As we are sent to fulfill Christ's Great Commission without trusting in our own gifts but knowing that we are sinners redeemed by the love and grace of God.

Johannes Tauler was a profound influence on Martin Luther. Of conversion Tauler wrote: "The soul has a hidden abyss, untouched by time and space, which is far superior to anything that gives light and movement the body. Into this noble and wondrous ground, this secret realm, there descends that bliss of which we have spoken. Here the soul has its eternal abode in the kingdom. Here a man becomes so still, so essential, so single minded, so raised up in purity, and more and more removed. This new state of the soul cannot be compared to what it has been before, for it is granted to share in the divine life." (Paul Althaus, *The Theology of Martin Luther*, pp. 79-89)

"God can cause our faces to smile even if things on the outside appear to be falling apart." – a thankful new convert.

Chapter Five
A Historical View of Conversion

At Vanderbilt University Divinity School, a history of preaching was required as a focus for the divinity program. A history of conversion from exploring past understandings before and since the Reformation shapes the present. Exploring the history shows the possibility that the church has conceived conversion in inadequate and unhealthy ways. The theologies of the past can be resources for today's church. There is potential to create the church's ability to lead people through the conversion process into mature eternal joy. Christians throughout the ages of history have chosen to participate in spiritual discipline. Jesus modeled and taught the essential discipline.

In later chapters, I will discuss spiritual formation. I found little help in literature that was written by Protestants. The first root is the Reformation. Insight is found in pietist and puritan tradition. I will address the contemporary use of spiritual formation in another chapter. Intelligent people with university connections and renaissance credentials wrote the 95 theses nailed to the Wittenberg church, Calvin's commentaries stirred the Reformation in England.

Martin Luther started the Reformation. He lived from 1483 to 1546. He never saw himself called to be a reformer. Luther conceived conversion through the lens offered by the church in his time. There were no guidelines to what being converted means. He realized that engaging in works of love and his faith did not rid himself of inner turmoil and uncertainty.

Pietists reacted against the scholasticism of the 16th century. They re-emphasized personal renewal, individual holiness, and religious experience. Pietists asserted a priority of spirituality over doctrinal debate. If the church is renewed, it takes godly people. They encouraged discussion of the Bible like the Moravians, who influenced Wesley.

When Jesus arrived for his earthly journey, the kingdom had also come. Jesus changed the understanding and expectation of what it meant to be the Messiah. He identified himself as the "suffering servant." Read Isaiah 53. Jesus changed the New Covenant from being a future event to the idea that the kingdom of God in the present time. These radical theological changes would be followed by others through the work of the apostles and evangelists in the first century. They spoke of experiencing the Holy Spirit. They also stressed the necessity of conversion that results in a new birth.

Luther said that a theologian must practice meditation, temptation, and prayer. John Calvin gives much space in his Institutes to the issue of self-denial.

Luther discovered it to be impossible to meet the conditions for salvation as stated by the state church. Condemnation and divine punishment brought fear. He felt his anger, anxiety, guilt, and fear, but never joy.

Critical to his work and ministry was developing a concept of conversion. Luther studied at the University of Erfurt focusing on the *via modern*, Latin for "the modern way." He embraced this theology before he rejected it. His embrace of this theology was reflected in his lectures on Psalms at the University of Wittenberg. Luther questioned the more works-oriented theology. He struggled to come to terms as he asked, "Is it possible for a person to prepare for conversion? "He also expressed concern with how a Christian perseveres in conversion to the attainment of perfect righteousness. Luther shifted away from the state church doctrine and the infallibility of the pope toward conclusions that would reshape Christendom's understanding of conversion.

Luther's opposition to the doctrine that one can earn salvation apart from the grace of God became stronger. His teaching was now expressed as a gift-centered theology. He opposed particularly the church tradition of selling indulgences. People believed that one could buy their way to salvation. He addressed this misconception in his 95 *Theses*. Selling indulgences is not an adequate means for conversion and that this is a false assurance of salvation. Justification was not something humans can buy, but a gift by grace and fait alone. His new language and vision are vastly different from the view of conversion reflected in the practices of the church. In Luther's conversion process, he viewed the Law as the way God led him into humility and desperation as he realized his sinfulness and inability to become righteous on his own.

Luther came to understand that we are made righteous by faith in Christ through free grace. God alone initiates conversion. All Christians have a right to the history of the church before the Reformation. It is pertinent history which is justification for using its historical riches. Christians need to become suspicious of denominational confessions or a church insisting on a particular form of the Christian life. In conceiving evangelism and conversion practices for the 21st century, the conceptions must not become a sausage machine, but as different as God's spirit makes them.

We could compose another thick book on the theology of conversion as expressed in history on to the relatively recent influence of modern revival influence on the church's practice of evangelization.

Charles G. Finney was converted at age 29. He was educated as a lawyer. His preaching was in a style of a lawyer making arguments to a jury. Finney rejected Calvinism, the predominant understanding in his community. His was a modified Arminian theology. He conceived of "new measures" in evangelism. He used an "anxious bench," where awakened sinners who were concerned about souls were instructed to come and sit.

Finney conceived conversion and evangelism theologically as a reaction against the Puritans. His ministry was in the 1870s and was practiced by D. L. Moody from the 1880's and 1890's. Billy Sunday preceded Billy Graham in using the practices of Charles Finney. Moody, Sunday, and Graham said nothing new about conversion. Graham was little known until William Randolph Hurst told his media empire to "puff Graham" during the 1949 Los Angeles revival.

Graham represents the essence of modern evangelism. Graham preached to more than 250 million people in person, face to face. His crusade sermons and other communications reduced the chance for theological depth. His urgent and oversimplified message failed to communicate the fullness of the kingdom of joy. The theme was always a gospel of forgiveness and assurance of heaven after death upon a profession of faith in Jesus Christ. Their goal was winning converts and using numbers as pride and power, not making disciples. Becoming a disciple was an optional further stage to commitment to Christ.

People who have experienced the joy of conversion will want to share their new reality with those living around them. Discipleship is the foundation, focus, and form of evangelism. We must "be" disciples to "make" disciples. Living as citizens in the kingdom of God, people cultivate credibility and an experience of joy. This joy ravishes with a vision of life in the kingdom with the fellowship of Jesus.

In the history of Christianity, countless churches hold a shrunken gospel distorting conversion and evangelism. Using the theological language words justification and sanctification, the church wisely invites people to interact with Jesus and the reality of the kingdom even before they come to believe.

In the current historical context, one problem is that we cannot seem to escape the individualistic concepts passed down through the ages. Evangelism in this century must challenge the socio-political realities of American society. The theology of churches, mainline, independent, or any other does not challenge the greed, racism, gross systematic injustice, sexism, classism, and any openness to that which now prevails in the culture.

Behind almost every tradition is a myth. Behind all traditions is that this is what people have always done, if not from time immemorial, or since our gathered group became the traditional culture. Church beliefs are always evolving whether we realize it. Forever means "as long as we can remember.' Often, this has not been long at all. Culture persists as it is essential for the cultural authenticity, which worships methods and old thoughts that are supposedly true to these timeless traditions.

The easiest and quickest way to destroy these illusions is to analyze the tradition and find how many are relative newcomers as we take the larger view of their histories. When church members say, "That's not traditional," that is disputable nearly every time. More interesting than mere "not as old as you think," is discovering how traditions have been constructed. The history of conversion is full of thoughts ossifying into timeless traditions.

It is tempting to get carried away with conceiving new spiritual ways. Any thoughtful writer can be disillusioned by the stories and experiences about how all traditions are not good or deep rooted. These must be helpful in spiritual discernment.

The long history of the Christian Church demonstrates God's faithfulness. Unlike the relative calm of the modern period, the early evangelists met severe opposition. Many were killed. None of us can minimize the way the church advanced trough reformation. The historical records of reform and spiritual revival are often fragmentary. Other events and historical news occupied the energy of historians. Reforms and evangelism methods were rejected.

A brief summary includes the centers of growth up to 300 as emperor Constantine made Christianity the official state religion. Irenaeus (175-195) led reforms in Lyons of Gaul. Montanism led to conversions in Asia Minor in the first to the third century. Gregory preached reform in Pontus. Another Gregory, the Illuminator, brought Christianity to Armenia in the third century. Martin of Tours (335-400), Saint Patrick (389-460) in Ireland, Augustine of Canterbury in England, Cluny and the monastic reforms, the Cistercians in the twelfth century, Francis of Assisi, Anthony of Padua, Peter Waldo and the Waldenses, John Wycliffe in England in the fourteenth century, John Millie, John Hus, Jerome of Prague, Girolamo Savonarola, Martin Luther (1483-1546, John Calvin in Switzerland, John Knox in Scotland, William Tyndale, Hugh Latimer, George Fox and those whom we will discuss later.

There were major awakenings after 1700. The Great Awakening happened from 1727-1780. The Second Awakening was in 1792-1842. The Third Awakening was called the great prayer revival from 1857-1859. The Fourth Awakening was considered a world-wide revival. The Healing Revival came with the Charismatic Renewal from 1948-1968, and the world-wide revivals from 1995-2020.The Great Awakening came to Germany with the Moravians. They had intimacy with God. They continued a prayer vigil for more than 100 years. Count Ludwig Von Zinzendorf was the leader of the Herrnhut Community or the Moravians. A revival was ignited at midnight during the Lord's Supper and the continuous prayer meeting. Moravians were known for their missionary work. They sent out more missionaries than all the denominations in the world had sent out in the preceding 250 years. The Herrnhut group never had more than 300 followers. They emphasized the power of praying without ceasing and being filled with the Holy Spirit.

The Moravians had an impact on the next revival in England under John Wesley and George Whitefield. Wesley experienced his conversion at a Moravian meeting where they were sharing the Preface to Romans. Wesley and Whitefield were the two most effective evangelists. Wesley was an Arminian and Whitefield was a Calvinist. The issues were if Jesus died for only the elect, or did he die for everyone. Was that election of God based on God's foreknowledge of an acceptance or rejection of the gospel or was it an unconditional election only on God's part? Could a person lose their salvation? During the years of my own ministry, I have served in 12 denominations with both Arminian and Calvinist roots. These theologies demonstrate two sides of conversion.

John Henry Newman (1801-1890) was influenced by Wesley. They both were Concerned about the moral and spiritual conditions in England. Both dispraised the ineffective ministries in the Anglican church. Wesley's approach was to take the gospel to the masses with a message of personal salvation and forgiveness. John Wesley moved people with emotion. Ecstasy overcame many of his converts. Some exhibited a suspension of normal consciousness and limitation of the sense organs. Later, many denominations of the Pentecostal kind departed from the Methodists. Conversion was called the immersion of the soul in God. The soul surrendered to God feels an internal reawakening and the inner fire of the presence of the Holy Spirit. John Henry Newman became increasingly opposed to this now established way of personal evangelism. Newman expressed concern that that it lacked appropriate dignity and reverence. He claimed again and again that any true and lasting religious experience could only be attained through proper church forms and rituals.

Newman graduated from the University of Oxford at age 19. His conversion came when he was 15. Four years later, Newman was ordained by the Church of England. He had rare abilities and a calming preaching style. He was a staunch evangelical, strongly opposed to the Roman Catholic Church. He went so far to say that the pope was the anti-Christ. Newman changed his direction preferring the ministers who promoted the idea of a high, liturgical church. He went to Italy to consult with leaders in the Roman Catholic Church about his personal spiritual struggles. He told them he wanted to see the Anglican church revitalized. During his trip, he became sick with a fever. He wanted to get back to England immediately. No transportation was available. Finally, a boat full of oranges was found ready to sail for France. For the lack of wind and a heavy fog the ship had to anchor. He was in tremendous physical, emotional, and spiritual despair. He cried out in prayer for God's guidance.

When he finally got back to England, Newman became the leader of the High church emphasis known as the Oxford Movement. They taught that the administration of sacraments as he only means of grace and salvation. Twelve years later, Newman broke completely with the Anglican Church and became a leader in the Roman Catholic Church. Pope Leo XIII named him a cardinal. (Kenneth W. Osbeck, *101 Hymn Stories*, pp. 150-156)

High Church became another way of doing evangelism, but the ways of the Great Awakening evangelists continued to influence the church.

The culmination of the Second Great Awakening was a mass meeting on the frontier in Cane Ridge, Kentucky. This revival began in the context of preparing for the annual communion celebrations among the Scottish Presbyterians which included Alexander Campbell. Church historians noted that the Holy Spirit fell upon them as it had in Cambuslang, Scotland while George Whitefield was leading. Before long, the word spread. People came from long distances by foot, horse, wagon, and train. Crowds rose until thousands were gathered. Within a year, one-fourth of all Christians in the American South had experienced a conversion.

The Cane Ridge revival drew so many people that there were not enough male preachers to meet the need. This was a time they began to use women preachers. During the Second Great Awakening, the largest, most influential churches would not allow a woman to preach. Some congregations were anti-intellectual, anti-authoritarian. They wanted nothing to do with the established churches.

It became impossible to have any control with the Cane Ridge Movement. The meetings were full of wild emotion. Converts cried out for mercy with loud voices. It was common to see people fainting to the ground. New converts would swoon and jerk uncontrollably. They barked like dogs. Our professor of the History of Preaching in America said their barking was to "tree the devil." (Deborah Peirce, *A Scriptural Vindication of Female Preaching*, pp. 12-15.

More than 100 women were involved with the preaching. They held meetings in barns, schools, brush arbors, and outside in the outdoors. Most female preachers at the time were lower class or poor. Despite their poverty, they said they were called. During the years of the Second Great Awakening churches flatly opposed female preachers. The reasons were biblical. They said it violated Paul's words in I Corinthians 14:34-35, "Let your women keep silent in the churches: for it is not permitted unto them to speak; but they are commanded to be under obedience, as saith the law." Churches then used only a King James Version. They also used Paul's words from I Corinthians 11:3 and I Timothy 2:11-12. In those days, they used the word "promiscuous" to describe mixed audiences. Some still speak of "mixed bathing" to refer to swimming. It also meant "licentiousness." The argument that women were inviting men to stare at them during public worship. Females could not violate the traditional of female modesty. Most women did not go to college. The High Church authorities feared that these congregations "quenched the spirit," by making a college education be a factor in ordination. Any farmer could be an expert on the Bible as somebody who had a degree from Yale.

Most new religious sects feared that the end of time was coming soon. They began to allow women to preach They urged every convert—man or woman—to spread the gospel before it was too late. William Miller, a farmer who made widely believed predictions such as that the world would end in 1844. Searching the Bible, they were moved by Joel's promise that "your sons and your daughters shall prophesy." Joel 2:28. Female preachers in the twenty-first century as well as during the awakenings would declare that instead of keeping silence, females such as Mary Magdalene, Priscilla, Phoebe, the four daughters of Philip had obeyed the Great Commission as witnesses and evangelists. Besides the Pauline warning "to keep silence in the churches was guidance for the disorderly women of Corinth.

Some female proclaimers caused controversy because they defended female evangelism. They were approved by their own sects. The novelty of seeing a woman in the pulpit drew crowds and "they listened with breathless attention to the heavenly story as it fell from her lips." Most female speakers prided themselves on preaching extemporaneously. That is why church historians cannot find any printed copies of their sermons. They were evangelical often speaking from John 3:3, "Ye must be born again." They insisted that men and women were equally created in God's image. However, there is not recorded that they shared the injustice and the early women's rights movement. They did not challenge the fundamental sexual inequalities within the church.

Most female ministers were single when they started their careers. Some divorced or left husbands. Some quit the pulpit after they married unless husbands supported them. Even though hundreds responded to them by professing their faith, they never asked for permission to baptize them or lead in the sacrament of communion or the Lord's Supper. Because they could not be ordained, they served as itinerant evangelists and were not appointed pastors. They were not paid, having to depend on their audiences for expenses. (Catherine A. Brekus, *Strangers and Pilgrims: Female Preaching in America, 1740-1845*, pp. 150-159)

They endured constant criticism and brutal harassment. People locked the doors to meetinghouses, booed them, labeled them as prostitutes. After the awakenings, women preachers faced more restrictions. Not only were they excluded from serving as preachers, but they were also erased from the pages of church record books. They were removed from historical memory. Despite their popularity, they were forgotten because nobody wanted to preserve their memory.

This tradition continued until the 1960's. When I was a seminary student at Midwestern Baptist Theological Seminary in Kansas City, there were but two female students. Today there are more women attending seminaries than men. These changing times have altered the ways the church does evangelism. Gifted women are no longer "strangers and pilgrims," but in many states in America and mainline denominations, most of the pastors are women.

Presbyterians and others established the New Light Christian in contrast to the Old Light Christian. The congregations moved from Calvinism and its five points: Total depravity, unconditional election, limited atonement, irresistible grace, and perseverance of the saints to Arminianism. Arminianism agreed with the doctrine of total depravity, but they also believed the atonement was limited to the elect and that election was conditioned upon a profession of faith. Arminianism made the assertion that Jesus died for all. They preached that there was not a particular atonement only for the elect, but a general atonement for whomsoever believes can be saved. Receiving the grace of God was a choice. Conversion did not violate the free will of anyone. They also taught the possibility of "falling away from" grace and losing salvation.

This theological shift split the Presbyterians. The Campbells had attempted to join the Baptists. And since the Campbells were Scottish Presbyterians, they attempted to join them. The Cane Ridge revival is considered the spot where the Restoration Movement resulted in the Church of Christ, independent Christian, and the Christian Church (Disciples of Christ) denominations. Baptists, Methodists, and Presbyterians wee prominent in the numbers involved in Cane Ridge. England was involved from 1740-1780 with John and Charles Wesley and George Whitefield with outdoor preaching and prayer with class meetings or home cells. Some historians believe this awakening saved England from a revolution like the one in France.

Through our disciplines that lead to intimacy with God, we understand that the best traditions are essentially alive and dynamic. As soon as anything stops living and become fixed as a cultural museum piece, it ceases to be tradition. It is then part of a historical heritage. In our search to know more about effective evangelism, the dynamics of conversion, some traditions might be revived. If so, it might not now be a traditional concept since it would no longer be tied to the past by continuous custom. It would be a self-conscious resurrection of the once dead practice. The meaning of conversion changes slightly in each era. Each iteration in each historical period is sufficiently alike that comprehension is not a problem. Theological word meanings are not fixed forever.

Unchurched people are aware of these unfortunate realities. Thousands have been deeply hurt by the people in the church. In the Body of Christ, pride, abuse, control, manipulation, abandonment, domination, and self-centeredness. Too many local churches are flooded with relational sins. The church is not always a haven from sin. Of course, the church is composed of sinners.

In unbinding the gospel, the church must recover the Good News Jesus preached, taught, and inaugurated in the life, death, and resurrection of Jesus.

Studying the historical concepts of conversion leads to a critique of modern evangelism and correction proposals that enriches today's church. Reframing the relationship between conversion, discipleship, and evangelism considering church history. Imagination must be awakened to divine insight. People are hungry for real life which is offered by God for the kingdom.

Music has always been a source of learning and being inspired. Songs in many congregations have shifted from classical structured worship based on hymns full of theology expressed in old words to an emphasis on transactional singing of love and devotion. Younger people tell us they believe they can worship better with the modern songs.

Families are more broken with personal problems abounding. Some assume that others are available to work with them on personal problems. Pastoral care and counseling have become a huge part of the ministry and this is significant. There is an increasing interest in the spiritual direction of young people, especially those who are attending college, a university, and or a theological institution. The movement asks the perennial question of how to view tradition in the light of the new ideas in the modern world. The pressures to not concentrate on finding new concepts are immense. The

Spirit of Joy Church has the happy but difficult task of allowing those rich roots of historical traditions to be considered in evaluations and direction in which the church has been blown away by contemporary movements in the contextualization that cannot be controlled.

Horace Bushnell and Washington Gladden emphasized spiritual formation. All of Bushnell's ministry was spent in just one church. His book on conversion, *Christian Nurture*, taught that a child should grow up a Christian and never know otherwise. Human personality development theory included speaking of infancy as the "age of impressions." Bushnell commented, "Let every Christian father and mother understand, when their child is three years old, that they have done more than half of all they will ever do for a child's character." (Horace Bushnell, *Christian Nurture*, pp. 200-201.) Bushnell spent time in his office where people sought his counsel. By this time in history, the rise of psychology of religion and the development of clinical pastoral education.

Washington Gladden wrote the hymn, "O Master, Let Me Walk with Thee." He used the word "friend" to describe himself. He said that a minister is a person in the community to whom anyone in need can turn to as a friend. Gladden co-operated with physicians as he believed there is a close connection between spiritual, mental, and physical health. Conversion to Christ brings health and peace. In 1899-1900 a class called "Psychology of Religion" was offered at Hartford Theological Seminary. Within ten years, the University of Chicago, Boston University School of Theology, Newton Theological School, Vanderbilt University School of Divinity, and Union Theological Seminary in New York provided such courses. (Gladden, Washington. *The Christian Pastor*, pp.240-249.

Anton Boisen, a Congregational pastor, had been a patient in a mental hospital. He was convinced that the church as not adequately ministering to those in the wilderness of the lost. With the encouragement and financial assistance from the medical community, Boisen established a chaplaincy program at Worcester State Hospital in Massachusetts which included clinical pastoral training. From this beginning the CPE (clinical pastoral education) is now an integral part of most theological seminary curriculum. This practical training is the most valuable influence in spiritual formation. By the eyes of a church congregation, the minister represents God.

The "long past" and the "brief history" of spiritual formation reveals a kinship with those moved by the Spirit of Jesus to be a neighbor to those lost in distress. God invites us to participate in the completion of the divine program for the world. God works through believers who are the image bearers. Humans are not spectators to what God is doing in the world. The fulfillment of the plan of God comes through our actions and efforts. Providence is the strongest incentive God gives us for vigorous activism. Prayer is essential. Still Christians must get off their knees to participate energetically in the answers to their own prayers. With a spirit of joy, all evangelists must with courage cross all sorts of cultural boundaries.

This boldness jars religious people out of their comfort zone. This means wrestling with doubts. It means not deeply sensing the love of God. It means not to be enabled to imagine why God does not step in and fix our troubles. We are earthbound. Facing a realistic concept of how life is in the moment makes us angry and full of grief. Little by little, discipline by discipline, God does get through despite our weaknesses. "The joy of the Lord" rarely is experienced as a supernatural ecstatic epiphany. God chooses to use the hands, prayers, and voices of image bearers.

When we dust for God's fingerprints, we discover the prints of an image bearer. We see only bits and pieces of what God is doing. Sometimes, we cannot see anything that enables us to make sense of what is going wrong in our lives. Dusting for traces of God yields no hard evidence.

Fruitful churches with a spirit of joy provide open opportunities for people to express their callings. They feel free to experiment with new ideas. They work to multiply ministry rather than to control it. They clarify the vision, identify the priorities, and set the boundaries for appropriate behavior. They allow people to self-organize and to be accountable to God.

Providence is the theological word that the church has historically attached to the teaching of how God governs the world. Providence assures us that there is much going on than what we see. God works behind the scenes to constantly move our lives in the direction of the divine goal. Providence is the way God loves, sustains, and governs the world. God had in mind a destiny for all creation. God never abandons the creatures to run alone. God enters an intimate relationship with creation. Providence is the focus on the activity of God in guiding the historical process to communicate God's intention for the created world. God's acts in history communicates a grand vision for the earth. This ambitious vision which involves God's children and a kingdom. Envisioning human beings to be like God, places enormous responsibility on us. This means as citizens of the kingdom on earth, we are to work, not as isolated individuals, but together. We are one body spreading the kingdom on this planet. During a vision quest at the Baptist Theological Seminary in Switzerland, Swiss Christians in Zurich shared the belief that God orchestrates everything in fine detail. Swiss reformer Ulrich Zwingli described the providence of God as so comprehensive as to encompass the activities of bugs, lice and fleas, flies, worms, roaches, and spiders. Reformation history reveals long held convictions about God's care proved ineffective in sharing the Good News.

Those in a Spirit of Joy church have been formed in uncomfortable directions. That is what reformers do. They upset the tidy views of God and divine involvement. The church of the cultures in church history tried to keep God at a comfortable distance from the awful events of life. If God makes only positive appearances, then we do not have to deal with the awkward questions about why bad things happen to good people. These thoughts were ineffective in sharing the kingdom of God then as they are now.

"Knowing the onramps to sharing joy, we strive fora deeper understanding of the power of the gospel." – John Piper

Chapter Six
Ineffective Evangelism in the Post-Christian World

The churches in the United States and much of the world are much less evangelistic today than they were just a decade ago. In most denominations, we are reaching non-Christians about half as effective as we were 50 years ago. In the early church "every day the Lord added to them those who were being saved." Acts 2:47. In most congregations today, the churches are reaching no one for Christ in the passing of an entire year.

Some churches are undertaking an effort to reverse their evangelistic stagnation. Thousands of churches are plateaued or declining. The church needs to reorder its priorities, refocus their vision, reclaim the mission, and lost the passion. Without a firm foundation, the church building will collapse on the members while they are sitting in the pews enjoying worship rather than experiencing God.

Churches have followed the pied pipers of a feel-good congregation and forsaken the joyful proclamation of the Good News. The Early Church performed miracles because the people believed. The living faith of the dead saints of God has been replaced by the dead faith of the cultural church.

On my Facebook page, I asked why we do such ineffective or no evangelism. Of all my Facebook friends, I had about 60 answers. One wrote, "Christians have no urgency to reach lost people." A Baptist pastor said, "Churches have lost focus on making disciples who will be equipped and motivated." A Church of God member said, "Most churches have unregenerate members who have never been converted." Several of my Christian Church (Disciple of Christ) colleagues thought, "Our churches have an ineffective evangelistic strategy of 'you come' rather than we go." In my research to write **The Joy of Prayer,** some observed "churches are no longer houses of prayer. We have become apathetic. Churches have retreated as culture becomes unbiblical and more like the rest of the world. Many Christians do not befriend and spend time with unchurched people. Many mainline congregations have a theology that does not encourage evangelism."

This revealed to me that here is concern about the lack of joy among Christians. One of my prayer partners prayed, "Lord, awaken us to our responsibility to obey the Great Commission. I pray the flame of evangelism fire will spread like Nebraska prairie fires."

More than two thousand years ago, a small band of men and women were set afire with the Lord's command. They were swept off their feet and carried away by the glory of such a visionary task. Within a short time after Pentecost, the fires of love and joy burned within every Christian. Acts 8:4 reported, "They that were scattered abroad went everywhere preaching the Word."

Since the beginning of Jesus' ministry, the need for individual conversion has been emphasized as a crucial experience in the lives of people. This need has been the emphases historically, especially in modern revivalism and the work of Charles Finney. The focus is the importance of an instant conversion using the method of deciding for Christ. Most mainline churches refuse to use that method. Most evangelical congregations institutionalized these aspects of modern revivalism.

This understanding has led churches to conceive of conversion through these thoughts on "instantaneous conversion" and a "decision for Christ." Except with anxious inquirers, instant evangelism was and is ineffective Its assumptions and methods fall short.

Samuel Southard referred to this concept as "instant evangelism." This meant an urgent need and individual appeal for salvation. The hearer is asked to make an immediate decision for Christ. (Samuel Southard, *Pastoral Evangelism*, Nashville: Broadman Press, 1962, pp. 24-26 and p. 40.)

These evangelistic efforts lack the ability to ignite conversion in the cultural context. That cultural context is shifting from Christendom to post-Christendom. Traditional evangelism methods have limited effectiveness in the new context. If Christians fail to fully grasp the current context where they minister and to adjust their evangelistic efforts, they will lose their ability to reach a growing portion of the population with the joy of living with and in Jesus.

The existence of church congregations is not for the insiders but for the outsiders. Whenever a church operates entirely for the benefit of those who already belong, it loses its focus and begins toward the process of closing. The Spirit works through the faithful church to form disciples of Christ. Jesus drew the attention of lepers, tax collectors, the poor, the Roman soldiers, the sick, the blind, the foreigners, and any seeking the meaning of life. Churches must invest energy, prayer, and focus on those outside the congregation more than those inside. Their evangelistic outreach is in welcoming visitors with upmost joy and delight.

Writing about the United Kingdom, Steve Hollinghurst observes, "Mission and evangelistic events are geared to those with church backgrounds, who were most of the population until about the 1900's. This has been true since the establishment of Christianity In Britain a thousand years earlier." (Steve Hollinghurst, *Mission Shaped Evangelism: The Gospel in Contemporary Culture*. Norwich: Canterbury Press, pp. 9-10) Hollinghurst relates that the churches in Great Britain have been fishing as always have in an old lake. The evangelism catch is not what is once was. The catch is shrinking. The methods once used are ineffective. The United Kingdom's fishing is designed for the lake populated by citizens raised in a Christian culture. The church has been losing children at a rapid rate. He thinks this trend will continue. Breaking this current pattern of long-term decline is not planned. The metaphor of the status of a fishing lake paints a bleak picture. Fishing in a new lake will bring better results than the old one. This important observation is that conversion and evangelism happen differently. Empirical evidence points to a drastically differing and mixed reality. Hollinghurst writes, "It is as if the few fish coming into the stock pond from the new lake are arriving without being caught by the fishing community." Ibid., 178.

Christendom is the common belief affirmed by consensus. What is orthodox in the minds is affirmed by religious and civic leaders. These views shape the politics, values, institutions, and terms of reference. This gives the followers of politicians a common sense of belonging. In the age of Christendom, the members of civil society and members of the church coincide perfectly. They called themselves the patriots. Society generates common behavior. Unlike the early centuries of the church, today the church reflects the common sense of those who are privileged.

Post-Christendom came in the collapse of ecclesial power. In modern America, the relationship between church and state has changed. Perhaps the state religion is the one where churches seem to worship conservative political leaders who say the right propaganda words. The church's influence is quite weak.

There is no longer a common belief system based on Christianity. There is no common belonging between civil society and members of the church. The church must figure out how to carry on its mission in this new world.

One problem with the current conception is that most just assume a Christendom context. When the church uses terms such as sanctification, justification, sin, God, faith, and hope, they presuppose that the audiences know what they are talking about.

As churches, mostly independent, insist on using the Word of God as authoritative, they think that non-Christians will accept the Bible as an infallible set of sacred books. For the most part, churches appoint and call pastors who have studied at accredited or university-based seminaries, so the context situation is not there. The gospel presentations, revivals, evangelistic practices come out of the Christendom context and assume that context is still present. The assumptions are no longer valid or effective.

The de-churched, who attended church before age 15, is shrinking and the non-churched is rapidly increasing.

Conversion with an immediate response seems to be the experience of the non-churched or those with a church background. Preaching with typical illustrations, preachers believe that the audience still has a context for understanding the message.

The cultural is changing. And few congregations are effective. Barriers are created for the children and youth that experience the conversion process. Some churches use summer Vacation Bible School as a bonanza for counting converts. The only converts and baptisms the church can report for a year are the summer Bible school kids. Realistically, these and the child evangelism workers are not effective with children.

Samuel Southard tells of a young pastor who decided to search more closely at the public invitations which he had been giving during Vacation Bible School. He gave his usual invitation for the children to accept Jesus as their Savior. This time he talked privately with each child who had "come forward to profess their faith." The pastor asked one why she came forward, he said, "Because Judy and Linda did." Another said, "I got tired of standing back there." A boy said, "I need to go to the bathroom." Still another reported,

"I just wanted to do what you said. I like you pastor." (Samuel Southard, *Pastoral Evangelism*, p. 91)

Southard noted, "The fruit of impatient evangelism is an incomplete conversion." More than half of the children from age eight to twelve, a year after Vacation Bible School were not active in any church. Some of the children in time looked with joy upon their early decision. Others have confessed that they "did not know what was going on" when they joined the church. One category pastors and evangelists use are a rededication and some request rebaptism. (Southard, pp. 92-94.)

How can these unfortunate understandings and practice be avoided? In the quest for truth, we discover the similarity of remarriage of divorced couples. In that remarriage and the rebaptism ceremony, the people are asking the church to repeat itself. In our new understanding of evangelism, an investigation of the reasons for a rebaptism or a remarriage might include the question, "How much have you grown up?" An ounce of prevention is worth a pound of cure. The best prevention of this problem is the cultivation of pre-marital and pre-baptism counseling. My wife and I did a six-week pre-marriage course as a requirement for those who are married at the Messiah Lutheran Church in Lincoln, Nebraska.

C. S. Lewis warned against churches expecting, even demanding, that newcomers to faith come in the exact same way, a one size fits all pattern. Conversion is rarely instantaneous or dramatic. One moment you are living in darkness, and the next moment you make a profession bringing forgiveness of sin, joy, and salvation. Coming down an aisle with "Just as I Am" or other moving music is affirmed as this fits the expected pattern. People who say that they experienced salvation as a process are treated with suspicion and doubt. That does not fit the pattern.

During a person's baptism time, expectations disallow us to see the saving grace of God at work. Some unchurched people lack the vocabulary and clarity to express God's activity in their lives. Sometimes I have baptized an entire family hearing a variety of conversion experiences that are biblical but not in terms they are accustomed to hearing. We cannot expect everyone to conform to a single pattern.

One ten-year-old girl, who had never been in a church sanctuary before, came to the front to listen to my children's sermon. I wore my colorful robe with a dazzling stole and doctor's degree bars on it. As she gazed into my eyes, she said, *"Are you Jesus?"*

After a couple of years of being active in church, she professed her faith, answered all leaders' questions, and was baptized as a disciple and church member. **"There are moments when I wish I could roll back the clock and take the sadness away, but I have the feeling that if I did, the joy would be gone as well." -- Nichols Sparks** Chapter Seven**Evangelism International**

Jesus said for us to "go into all the world." As the World Evangelist for the United Methodist Evangelism Council, Eddie Fox has traveled to nearly 100 nations. The World Methodist Council has developed a program called "Connecting Congregations." During recent years, George Morris and Eddie Fox have given their faith-sharing principles in countries on every continent. (Eddie Fox and George Morris, *Faith-Sharing*, pp. 2-3)

Evangelism means proclaiming the gospel to all people. That word gospel is a combination in English of "good spell" meaning "good news." The spreading of good news of Jesus Christ including the use of all means of action for reaching out to all people groups. The Great Commission is the great obligation of the church. Read Romans 10:14-15. Paul stresses the question of sin and separation from God. Read Romans 3:10-18. Through repentance God meets human sin and offers to restore individuals to wholeness in the image of Christ. Repentance is the first step. The author of Psalm 72 announces the fulfillment of promises given to Abraham. In the prayer for the righteous king, the psalmist describes a king whose rule of peace and justice included all people living on earth. All nations could be covered by God's blessings. The writer also explains that the king would deliver all nations, fulfilling their needs, and blessing every one of them. Isaiah 9:6-7 says the same.

Isaiah prophesized the evangelization of the world in the servant songs. Read Isaiah 42:6-9; 49:6, 52:13-53:12. The servant of the Lord will bring the joy of international salvation.

This found fulfillment in the early church. The apostles and scattered believers from Jerusalem preached the gospel first to the Jews. That preaching offered the promised opportunity for everyone who would call upon the Lord to be saved. No direct New Testament reference refers to promises given by the prophets such as Jeremiah 4:2 or Zechariah 8:13. The many indirect connections were made in the preaching of the apostles that the nations of the world would receive the blessings of God through Israel's faith.

After the resurrection, the disciples received a clear sign that the restoration had started. Jesus informed the disciples that he had all authority in heaven and on earth. With that authority he sent them into the world to make disciples of all nations. Matthew 28:19-20. Jesus transformed the understanding of the kingdom including the Gentiles. With his teaching he fulfilled the promise to Abraham that through his seed all nations would be blessed.

The disciples received the Holy Spirit on the day of Pentecost. They were slow to disperse among the nations to share the joy. As we read the first seven chapters of Acts, the movement did not spread beyond Jerusalem. Peter received specific instructions about this witnessing in Caesarea while he was in the house of Simon in Joppa. Read Acts 10:19-20. God sent Peter to Cornelius, an influential Roman centurion who wanted to understand how to fulfill God's will and to receive the joy of God's favor. The Holy Spirit convinced the apostle to share the gospel without distinction of origin or culture. The Holy Spirit transformed Paul's understanding of the Old Testament Messiah that had come from Paul's training by the noted scholar Gamaliel. Paul made three missionary journeys covering the eastern part of the Roman Empire. During his first journey, the Holy Spirit widened his understanding to include Gentiles. Read Acts 13:46-51. On his second journey, Paul traveled to Europe, reaching in Macedonia and Achaia. Read Acts 16-18. The third missionary journey expanded the outreach with a three-year stay in Ephesus. Read Acts 19:9-11.

After Paul was imprisoned, the concerted disciples from Ephesus continued to evangelize the people around them. Read I Timothy 1:1-7. Paul reached out not only to ordinary people but also rulers and kings. Read Acts 23-27. The Church is identified as a servant helping the world to be freed from any bondage that makes people ignorant of the saving love of God. The church is still trying to find ways to communicate as the world changes. The early disciples took the gospel and spread it as far as they could go. Proclaiming the Word to all the world was Jesus' command. Evangelism fulfilled the promises that Jesus told the apostles regarding the Holy Spirit. Read John 14:16-17.

The Great Commission did not stop after the death of the early Christians. This body of Christ offers spiritual nurture, makes disciples of Christ, and provides physical help by caring and supporting people in their needs. Jesus humbly said that the disciples who come to serve in all times and places, would do even more miraculous things than he did.

After my emersion into the meaning and power of joy, I felt affirmation as Dr. Norman Vincent Peale anointed me the Minister of Joy to the World during one of his Schools of Practical Christianity. After nearly 70 years of ministry, I have now shared the joy of the Lord on all seven continents. I have spent most of my money in this miraculous adventure. Often, I stay in homes of missionaries, members of the military, or in hostels and hotels during tours of the world.

A few years back I went to share my joy-based message in Cuba. A group of Cooperative Baptists organized the trip to connect with Cuban congregations. Some of the church buildings were in the *campo* or as Baptists might call the church in the sticks. The meeting room for worship was about as big as my home office from which I am composing this book. There was a hard cement floor sanctuary. The walls were bare. The chairs for the people were those plastic lawn chairs with damaged seats. There was no piano, no organ, no harp, and no musical instruments. The Cuban pastor said, "We only use our voices." With tears, we thanked God for those believers worshipping from that place.

People in churches throughout the world spent time thinking about what they do not have. Like those faithful Cuban believers, we need to think about what we do have. I am thankful for having heard choirs from many nations representing various cultures and ethnicities. Those videos renew my mind about the creativity and unique international evangelism. C.S. Lewis said, "In such a fearful world, we need a fearless church. "This world needs a continuing reformation. The Reformation did not end in the sixteenth century. That was just the beginning. No person or institution can control God or speak for God. Faith is not a complicated belief system. Martin Luther spoke fearlessly, "We are saved by grace through faith." Redemption is not the right doctrine. Luther helped start something. Later, the reformers became the enforcers. The Reformation must go on. The Holy Spirit never stops sharing something new. The Spirit does not help us keep a static, stubborn, unyielding way. The Spirit's way is to urge, invite, indicates in a dynamic process. We must keep thinking, keep finding new ways to do evangelism, and keep discerning what God is doing. No one way can claim to be the only way. Words are cheap if they are not rooted in actions. We must continue to be open to God who is wiser, more graceful. Nothing is up to us.

Reforming the church cannot happen until we take time a be grateful for what we do have to fulfill the Great Commission. God's presence is the greatest resource in whatever nation the gospel is shared. God has deposited distinct reflections of glory into the differing ethnic groups and cultures of the earth. In each culture there are things that honor God. We learn so many valuable things from the sisters and brothers in Christ anywhere we travel. When I observe how the church hierarchy devalues the older people and the retired ministers, I know Asian Christians honor elders. South Sudanese disciples rejoice even during terrible tribulations. Latin American Christians take care of family in their culture. They support far extended family which we are aware of in the immigration struggles. As we reflect on evangelism, we discover what we learn from differing cultures. We must surrender our own plans to be open to the vision of God. Multi-cultural international evangelism is the desire of God.

We share faith not just for the sake of the church but for the people with whom we share. My evangelist roots are sensed in a practical Christianity in an arena for living discipleship. The alarming truth is that evangelism is dying inside the church, not merely outside of it.

Evangelism is not carried out by people sent overseas. It is part of the local church. Some congregations go on long foreign mission trips with youth every year. Some singing groups constantly are traveling to share the joy of music. Evangelism is natural for the church wherever it is located. This fundamental and creative way of thinking combats the issue of professionalism. Those who lead international mission trips see danger in allowing their congregation to claim their missional dimension in all activities by laying on the occasional outreach trips to fulfill its evangelistic intention. This would be self-justifying and would perpetuate the problem.

As a student at Carson-Newman University, I served as a summer missionary sponsored by the Baptist Student Union and the Home Mission Board of the Southern Baptist Convention. Intentional evangelism must not be sub-contracted out of the church to mission boards alone. That removes an essential ingredient from the nature of the church. As young students we did

10 revivals and 12 Vacation Bible Schools during this journey to places far away from home.

One fresh evangelism approach is the raceway ministry at the speedways. When I served as pastor for Saint Luke United Methodist Church in Bristol, Virginia, we joined with other churches in giving out free food and drinks out of a tent. We worked late into the night to be available to share the joy of the Lord with those attending the races. At least two or three people would die among the 200,000 race fans each tear. We would minister to those grieving families at the hospitals. The owner of the raceway even gave us a place for worship nearby.

Another unique and effective ministry was the College World Series ministry in June each year in Omaha, Nebraska. Clinics for youth were given by major leaguers. A banquet is held for the eight teams in the NCAA tournament. For the fans, we gave out cold water in bottles with a scripture about knowing Jesus and never thirsting again. It is usually hot as Nebraska has just two seasons . . . shovel and swat.

There is a troubling debate over where and how God is redeeming the world. The discussion has been ongoing between evangelicals and the ecumenical movement. Mainline churches discuss also how God is working in other religions. The church must be selective in its response to changes in the society. It embraces some certain changes; it may subvert and reject others.

Preaching and teaching about evangelism and missions has been lost in most congregations. The sad result is seen everywhere Most believers cannot define what an evangelist or missionary does in relation to the Great Commission.

Each Christian has a genuine contribution. The Great Commission is a call for participation at the grass roots level. This brings a sense of belonging that allows the outsider in finding faith and an effective community. The implication is that the evangelistic activity of the church is dependent on the participant. If they default, then that activity causes the church to have to default.

In the New Testament, Jesus was to some extent dependent on the participation of those who explore his testimony. He could not have done his evangelism without the hospitality of support of Martha and Mary, Zacchaeus or Peter's family.

Any congregation responding to cultural changes must be flexible and adaptive. One movement in recent days is the Emerging Church for Fresh Expressions. That movement tries to embrace changes in order to be an example where evangelism finds its place in the heart of the church.

The Emerging Church for Fresh Expressions does church in the culture of the people involved as opposed to conceive and designing church in the language of those who already have been converted. If the church values transforming secular space by identifying with the life of Jesus, then the expectation of a life of mission.

Taking the Good News to other nations includes being open to learning something new from authentic encounters. Some expressions of the Emerging Church cater to Christians disillusioned with church. Some are experimenting with worship and liturgy and seldom use the e-word. The Emerging Church is one model of how the church could respond to some of the objectives to current evangelism practices.

Christians in the world have quadrupled from about 600 million in 1910 to more than two and a half billion today. Roman Catholics is the largest denomination with 1.3 billion. There are now more than 44,000 denominations. Brazil has the largest number of Catholics with 140 million, more than Italy, France, and Spain combined. The ten most dangerous places to be a Christian are North Korea, Afghanistan, Somalia, Pakistan, Sudan, Eritrea, Yemen, India, Iraq, and Iran. (Center for Global Christianity at Gordon-Conwell Theological Seminary.)

Evangelism cannot be disregarded due to past embarrassments. Imaginative leadership is critical, and that issue has not been addressed. The Great Commission is the foundation for international evangelism.

If the current church refuses to be a light to the world, the Lord will take the candlestick away. Pretending the poor and lost do not exist is one alternative. Averting our eyes and ears from the truth will not eliminate our guilt and shame. The church of Jesus exists to remind the affluent, the top dogs, the powerful, and the greedy that there is a needy, hungry lost world of human beings out there whom Jesus loves and for whom he lived and died. Read II

Corinthians chapters eight and nine. We must repeat and repeat again what God's vision is. Paul urged wealthy Christians for support and for collecting resources and money for the poor congregations. The New Testament shows that Jesus made himself poor for the salvation of those who are so spiritually desperate. Most of the world is homeless, naked, and hungry for the sake of Christ.

God's vision of the Great Commandment and the Great Commission is not to sleep along roadsides and sharing in the orphanages and prisons but to share with practical Christianity through financial sharing and intercessory prayer.

During World War II, the allies showed themselves capable of huge sacrifices. Soldiers and civilians live on meager and poor rations. They defeated dictators and Nazis, the Italians thinking they would create a new world. History repeats itself as American Nazis, the KKK, and soldiers for hire plan how they can accomplish the same greedy goals. See II Timothy 2:3-4. These are critical times, perhaps more so with the deep divisions in the culture.

How we share or refuse to share our resources is a barometer of a nation's spiritual strength. Withholding hospitality and refusing to share a common table are clear signs of hostility. Current global trade rules do not reflect a warm international conviviality. In place of sharing, there is a limited form of charity from the rich to the poor. A flaw in our American kind of government is that the rich gain and the poor lose. There is no equality. Rich countries make it harder for poor nations to export what they have. This results in trade barriers. Our elected congress persons and the powerful president becomes shallow, hedonistic, and egotistical. In any perception, we need to realize that we should be in service to one another. That is the way the world can live together in peace and joy. We are all fragile, mortal, fleshly beings who are stiving to survive.

Without continuous conversion, life is absurd. It is the meaning of Camus' *Myth of Sisyphus*. Sisyphus is condemned by the gods forever to push a heavy stone up a hill, only for it to roll back down to the bottom every time. Sisyphus can only be happy if he embraces his fate, which is pointless. In dark, negative perceptions, we are condemned to chase and catch a greased pig. During the Cass County Fair in Nebraska, daring people got their hands around but never kept hold for just a few seconds. The futile games leave us standing in a pen with nothing to do.

The traditional alternative is worse. Traditional puritans renounce the pleasures of the flesh. They try to embrace the satisfactions for their soul. The promises of eternity. We must turn to God to transcend pathetic human limitations, and seek instead the kingdom of God, a world without end, where we know unlimited joy.

What the world has experienced in 2020 is another deadly event. Missionaries throughout the world have remained active and creative in obeying the Great Commission. Because of my international sharing of joy in Visionquests, many Christian ministers correspond with me. With today's technology, I continue to connect by email, Facebook, telephone, websites, and Zoom videos. Prayers fuel Evangelism International enabling us to update each other on what God is doing through believers.

In developing nations, we will never know how many died from Coronavirus, because the numbers are less by those who have from starvation. In a host of countries there is no access to basic medical resources because of lockdowns.

God is not only at work even in this darkness. The dark nights have removed the distractions in the world, so Christians can shine brightly in the darkness of pandemic Covid-19. This virus caught the whole world off guard, bring confusion, anguish, despair, and pain. Hospitals were overwhelmed, worship places were closed, and the economy fell apart. Nothing could be compared, not earthquakes, landsides, droughts, hurricanes, or fires. In those disasters, people know what they must deal with, know what to do, and how repair the damages later. Nobody knows what do now. We do not know when it will be finished.

We pray that all people understand how fragile life is. God is the only one who can give us light and hope in this time of distress. An evangelist and pastor shared the birth of new church congregations in the diseased world. Peter Rong, a graduate of the Baptist Theological Seminary in Bucharest, planted the Spiritual Revival Baptist Church in Bucharest to reach the ethnic groups represented in this city of nearly four million population. The church faced the pandemic that sneaked its sinister tentacles as Romanians fled out of Italy. The Romanian journalists noticed and honored the church. The church began to organize with digital alternatives for worship. Applications such as Zoom, YouTube, Skype and others allow the family to connect in an intimate way. They videotaped sermons and music teams led in worship. They videoed from their homes. The church began to simulcast in English, Caching, Farsi, French, and Romanian. What a clear picture of sharing Christ Jesus' Great Commission was this newly planted congregation that performed a miracle during a difficult time. God has made us an artist for change. Miracles of doing evangelism happen anywhere as we watch the way of rain when it falls slow and free.

We who are living in the pandemic years talk about the difficulties of our times as though we must wait for better days before the Christian faith can flourish amazingly in unfavorable conditions.

Most change takes place slowly. Crunch time arrives when we think God is not doing something now. More change come from a crisis than intention. The Holy Spirit keeps nudging to create and act on new thoughts. Not acting squeezes back into past ways that do not work. The Spirit awakens the body of Christ to free the possibilities in eternal time. This awakening strives to suggest the silent depths that have been hiding in the dark. The grace of God is the permanent climate of emerging springtime into the winters of bleakness.

God's unchanging and unconditional love allows the dawn of new understanding. Understanding nourishes in the shelter of the Spirit. In the post-Christian, post-modern era, the world is hungry to find and share Good News. All the possibilities of our destiny are still asleep in many souls. When the love of the Spirit becomes fresh and new, there are unrecognized paths to eternal living in the kingdom.

The early Christians were on fire with the conviction that they were the sons of God with their brother Jesus. I believe that realizing how they turned the world upside down would give us insights. Those early believers emphasized repentance as turning away from evil and turning to god through salvation in Jesus Christ. They also proclaimed the beginning of the kingdom of God.

Today and for decades the church emphasized conversion "in order to get to heaven." They preached, "Repent for the kingdom of God is near." If we find a way to be effective is by developing an atmosphere of joy that is encouraging, welcoming, and empowering. Evangelism is sharing faith with others who are disconnected from the reign of God. We invite them to follow Jesus as disciples. Faithful congregations receive new people upon their testimony and profession of faith, and not only the transfers from other churches.

One essential in a new vision for evangelism is to note that God is responsible for conversion. We believers are responsible for making the gospel known. We are not responsible for making new converts. We do not have that authority or power.

The church can relax and stop worrying about results. Releasing the responsibility for conversion give us the insight that evangelism is never something we do for people. Evangelism is making the gospel known. We must stop believing that conversion is always instantaneous.

In the testimony of my own conversion, and the conversions of others, I believe there are four elements. Those include belief, repentance, trust and assurance of salvation, and commitment as we get to know Jesus and to become determined to live for him. These are internal realities. Outward signs included baptism, the gift of the Holy Spirit, and membership in a Christian community. To be converted results in a lifestyle that follows Jesus out into his mission.

"Joy is what happens to us when we allow ourselves to recognize how good things really are." –Marianne Williamson

Chapter Eight
Living the Vision of God

What if we saw ourselves as God envisions us? Before we ever drew breath, God created us for a purpose. God's personal vision that is beyond our limited perspective. If we could see with God's eyes, we would see an earthbound life with a much wider heavenly perspective.

We were created as children of God, not children by chance. Why are we here? Living the vision of God, we strive in a close, loving relationship with God. As we look beyond our present circumstances, we gain awareness of God within as the Lord oversees every moment. We need a pair of spiritual lenses to see it. The lovely Irish song, "Be Thou My Vision," has inspired me. It continues to lodge in my soul with a spiritual rapture: "Be thou my vision, O Lord of my heart; naught be all else to me, save that art thou my best thought by day or by night, waking or sleeping, thy presence my light."

And the fourth verse captures God's vision: Great God of heave, my victory won, may I reach heaven's joys, O bright heaven' s Sun! Heart of my own heart, whatever befall, still be my vision, O Ruler of all."

This eighth century hymn was sung at my ordination as an elder in the Holston Annual Conference at Lake Junaluska, North Carolina. It is sung at many reviving Vision quest for Joy meetings. (Mary Byrne, trans, "Be Thou My Vision," *Chalice Hymnal,* hymn number 595)

Often a pianist or organist plays it softly at the end of the gathering. Jonathan Swift wrote, "A vision is the art of seeing things invisible. Peter Marshall prayed, "Give us clear vision that we may know where to stand and what to stand for, because unless we stand for something, we shall fall for anything." Katherine Logan noted, "Vision is of God. A vision comes in advance of any task well done." The first association with this hymn was in the *Irish Church Hymnal,* published in 1919. The tune "With My Love on the Road" was used by Saint Patrick challenging King Loegaire and the Druid priests as he lit a Paschal fire. The melody has been harmonized by a host of musicians. Another anonymous writer has penned some significant thoughts about the importance of having a vision: "A vision without a task is a dream; a task without a vision is drudgery; a vision with a task is the hope of the world." (Kenneth W. Osbeck, *101 Hymn Stories*, pp. 10-12) The word vision is a noun.

A vision can be a thing seen and a sense by which a thing is seen. The Irish hymnist is asking God to become what can be seen. She is asking God to appear before her. She is asking God to be her vision. That is what she says in the final stanza: "waking or sleeping, thy presence my light." "Be thou my vision" is like the command of the Great Commission. The hymn illuminates a deep truth about understanding God as our vision. Envisioning the Great Commission is a spiritual journey of asking questions and receiving answers. Living the vision of God brings a spiritual awakening, allowing yourself to be open and inviting the living Spirit of God and the love of God enter your inner self. It awakens the soul to a new awareness, a new perception of the world around you. You will begin to feel more sensitive and feel more empathy for others. If you are experiencing more synchronicities, signs, numbers, and omens, that is God.

A vision statement captures in words a picture depicting the future. It comes out of the present reality as it is being lived. A vision statement paints a picture of a positive, hopeful state of living. Congregations ask, "Where is our church heading?" As pastors we are responsible for leading in the power of the Spirit to help the entire body of the church to live in the vision. The vision statement must align with you and your church's passion, graces and gifts. The ministry represented by the congregation needs to operate in harmony with the vision.

God's vision for our lives is the heartbeat that pumps through our purpose. God reveals the vision over time. As we respond to what God reveals, we begin to live in the vision of God.

In some of my Visionquests in international evangelism, people have shared their dreams and visions through which God takes the message, especially where there are little or no Bibles or translations in their group language. As God desires to communicate with a group, anything can be used such as a dream, a vision, or an angel, or a missionary. There is no limit to what God can accomplish.

If you believe you have had a vision from God, prayerfully examine the Bible to make sure your vision agrees with Scripture. In your time of prayer and searching, consider what God would have you do in response to the vision. James 1:5. Our loving God would not bring a vision and then keep the meaning of the vision hidden. Daniel 8:15-17.

Having a vision from God is essential to our future if we expect to reach our destiny appointed by God. All during my life journey, God has guided me in relation to my ultimate destiny. If we stop and consider our forefathers in faith, we see a similar pattern of how God worked in their lives. With all my experiences, I realize that vision give us staying power. Vision gives me strength and endurance to press on when life is difficult. I stop and think about where I am today. Seeing is believing and receiving. We cannot receive what we cannot perceive or have a vision for. Envisioning clears the future with our natural eyes. Envisioning it with spiritual eyes vision is realized face to face with God.

Living the vision of God includes times of quietness and prayer when we are alone with God. How many times in the middle of prayer has God spoken? A God gives a vision everything disappears. We are now looking at a movie screen or a video and we sense a particular thing taking place. In Jeremiah 1:11-12, the word came to Jeremiah as he saw an almond branch. God told him, "You have seen it well, for I am watching over my word to perform it."

Having a clear vision, spiritually or physically is necessary for us to move in the right direction. When Jesus healed and restored the sight of a blind man, he asked him if he could see. Mark 8:3-25. In this confusion and difficult time when a pandemic is raging, God wants to restore our ability to keep in tune with visions in times past, and to bring them into sharp focus so we can move into our destiny. Living in the vision of God requires us to walk in a perpetual state of faith and expectancy. God shifts the things of life suddenly.

One who attended my quest for vision said, "Thanks for the deep insight into vision. I am so blessed by your teaching. There are several issues bothering me concerning what God has shown me and I do not want to mistake it for vision. I want to share it with you for further guidance."

Our vision quest builds on our purpose. Purpose clarifies. Vision motivates. Purpose is the reason we are living on our earthly journey. Vision is joy songs we sing. Purpose anchors us. Vision releases imagination. Purpose gives meaning to living. Vision demands action. A motivating vision pictures God's preferred future.

Some discerning questions that will reveal the intensions of the future can be asked. Is the vision clear to anyone who reads it or hears it? Will the vision inspire the congregation or even the denomination to take steps toward making the vision a reality? It is a challenging vision? Do the words line up with what we know is God's will and with scripture? Read John 14:1-14.

Finally, will this vision outlive us? An effective vision statement will stimulate effective evangelism. Visions exist for the common good. Repeat it in the newsletter, the website, anywhere the vision is kept visible for all who might be involved in ministry. Share stories of tangible ways in which the vision is being lived and realized. The strategies for achieving the vision may change.

Worthy visions drive people to their knees. There is a joyous element to them that overwhelms. Living the vision of God is larger than what can be realized by mere mortals.

The Spirit of Joy Church with its vision from God to create an atmosphere where joy and miracles happen as we share the Good News with the world. We have all been called to as disciples to spread the joy of the Lord throughout the earth. "Rejoice with me, for I have found my lost sheep that was lost." Luke 15:6. Our personal testimony looks like a daunting task as more of our years unfurl and life is now viewed with the benefit of hindsight. How can we testify about the story of life with God? As my conception of conversion involves ultimate joy, I have known God's grace in the hardest places. By God's grace, I saw into my past with eyes that looked beyond the confusion and the dark days. I felt free. I recall the joys from childhood to older and final years. My soul leaps in recognition as I envision God within. I love to testify on being a recipient of grace. I become the broken clay pot receptacle of God's presence. The task of becoming Christ-like is rarely taken as a serious objective. Jesus made it clear that nobody was a servant of the body or the flesh would succeed. Sinful practices become habits, then they become a choice, and finally it is ultimate characters. Christian formation is the redemptive process of forming the inner human world so that it takes on the character of the inner being of Jesus Christ himself. The outer life becomes a natural expression or overflow of the character and teachings of Jesus. Spirituality is not a passive process. Being like Christ in living is not a human achievement. It is a gift of grace. It includes the interactive presence of the Holy Spirit and the spiritual treasures stored in the body of Christ in the world today.

There is no formula for spiritual formation. It means a dynamic relationship that is individualized. Christianity is at a crucial point in the progress of the

Christian faith. A door of opportunity is currently open for us and we must not miss it.

There were no creeds or scriptural stories when the church was born. The New Testament was not written when the call for evangelism started. The New Testament is a record of how the church did its work. Evangelism ignited the growth with God's Word. In the Spirit of Joy every member serves as an evangelist. As they shared within the gathered group, they go into the hostile world outside.

Today the church focus is to serve the faithful, not to make disciples. The result is decline in church membership. We need to return to create a vision from God. In prayer the local and gathered conceive a vision that centers on Christ. The early Christians knew who and what they were. There is silence in the church in vital areas of living such as basic beliefs, prayer, sexual abuse, the theology and spirituality of joy. The modern congregations cause the unchurched to view them as irrelevant. Evangelism is not just the means of spreading Good News. It is living the vision of God. Living for the moment is not enough. Life is not just one moment. It may be viewed as comprising moments. It is not a series of moments Life is a pattern composed of relationships in each moment. The difference between spending a year enjoying one experience after another, ticking off the bucket list of things to do before we die. Time is made of moments, but the whole of life is greater than the sum of its parts. A relationship is built from days together, but it is more than a collection of days. This book is made up of hundreds of words, but it is more than a collection of words. We live in the present. Still we need to look for guidance from our past to discern the vision of God. The past is a record of how God has shaped us. As we "listen" to our life and our congregation's life, the Holy Spirit will give us clear insight into what we need to understand. This is the way we discern past, present, and future. Learn from the past, envision the future to live our vision in the present.

God's vision for the future is anticipated in the past. I have found it helpful to create a timeline of my life, the life of a congregation, or even the historical life of the church. Reality shows at if we felt up, a down time came later. If we record a down time, we usually have a following up time. In the reflection of a lifetime, common threads and patterns emerge. We gain insight to how God has shaped us for a unique purpose. Ask a visioning person or group about the common themes. These reveal how God has worked during your life. This kind of discerning exercise makes clear what God has been forming in us for the future. Having the keys to the kingdom of God is not just controlling access to the kingdom. Keys do not mean the right to control access. Imagine a woman who carefully kept her apartment door locked. She has the correct key to get inside, but never entered her own home. Living the vision of the kingdom is what counts.

Kierkegaard was on point about conversion as "a matter of becoming as contrasted with being." It is not a condition, that one just settles into, but an ongoing life process of continuing to become. Conversion is a verb disguised as a noun. **The Vision Quest**

Write down what you believe is the vision of God. The quest to articulate a vision represents your best understanding of God's motivating vision. It may not be a final understanding. You might state the vision in another way at some later date. The vision comes clearer as we obey and see the issues that must be addressed as the church breaks the silence on issues important to God and the world. The essential ministering to a hurting and lost world face as no longer ignored.

One taboo area largely disregarded in churches is Christian sexual morality. *The Silence of the Church: The Spiritual Struggle with Sexuality* faces this hurdle, shared in 2017 by Parson's Porch Books. Violence and injustice make mockery of the value of human life. Divorce is common. The laws made in congress are made from selfish greed and drive for power without a thought about Christian principles. Envisioning the will of God is not just to maintain faith with no future. My Spirit of Joy Church conception brings hope to avoid extinction. Ephesians 4:4 informs us, "There is one body and one Spirit, just as there is one hope to which God has called you."

In a book by Martha Reese, *Unbinding the Gospel*, she writes, "Life with Christ is reality. It is joy. It is hope. It is salvation It matters more than anything. This is the heart of faith. This is the good news." (Martha Reese, *Unbinding the Gospel*, p. 105.) Living the vision of God requires internal reflection not external ones. Having no vision is the cause of no efforts to share with unchurched who regard the church with apathy. These lost ones will search in other places for spiritual food. Aging members (most churches have mostly over age 50 members) find that they cannot attract their own children and grandchildren. "Where there is no vision, the people perish." Proverbs 29:18.

Without ongoing reflection and recommitment to living God's vision, the faith community will die. The quest for vision inspires, steers, motivates, clarifies, facilitates, and creates a reformulation. Just like the first-century church, the Spirit of Joy church is a mission outpost. Differing outposts serve different segments of the unreached, and in combination with one another, is the key to ministering to people of all ages, all races, all economics, and in all nations. This is the living vision of God.

I have shared the vision that I live by in my ministry, home life, and enjoy. Other people's visions can help us refine our own statements. One vision reads: "I know God desires to use me to offer our children the spiritual, emotional, relational, experiential, and financial resources they need to become disciples, to grow in faith, answer God's call, and make their own unique contributions as adults."

A teacher wrote: "I know God has placed me as a public schoolteacher so I can be a source of light to others and I can offer my students a chance at a better life."

Another vision statement: "God has given me a vision to build a congregation passionately committed to the goal of reproduction of disciples, leaders, groups, ministries, and sites. My role is to model reproduction and to make it the highest possible priority in my ministry."

Some declining or dead congregations cannot be turned around. Their organizational structure is locked in the past. Changes that would be expected are threatening. Without a vision, the church will never become one that envisions the Great Commission as the essential thing.

Congregations unwilling to follow the leading of the Spirit become isolated and afraid to break free of a comfort zone. They do not have the energy to connect or relate to those cut off from knowing love. They hold resentment from the past. It is not easy to let go. In contrast to a Spirit of Joy Church, they feel guilty, angry, anxious, fearful, and full of stress.

The current church ruled by the so-called two percent will not be abandoned. A few of my own vision quests has been on cruises. Once the ship moves out to sea, a change of direction cannot be made easily, but comes into existence with a new direction and pressure of the ninety-eight percent is applied.

During my pastoral work, I had the congregation repeat their vision frequently. I used in my sermons, in board meetings, at our church dinners, and in support groups with fellow ministers. We used it in our communication channels. We used a weekly church newsletter, *The Weeping Water Word and Way*, to bombard people to live the vision. It was sent by e-mail with minimal finance. Unless the vision of a Spirit of Joy congregation is relentlessly repeated, it will not take hold.

The two percent who are the real leaders get uncomfortable with the new joy brought by new members. It means the closing of a familial atmosphere in the church, or a lessoning of older members' sense of belonging. New people bring uncertainty and change. To continue the growth power must now be shared as will the perceived importance of established members. The new vision brings an unwelcome competitor for time and funding. Any congregation that lacks the joy that comes with outreach should consider whether they have strayed from the Great Commission.

I read many books on evangelism at Vanderbilt and Yale Divinity Schools. Yale had a Templeton Foundation grant of several million dollars. I received more insight into joy the last few years as I traveled to New Haven to listen and learn. In a youth ministry seminar, the facilitator said, "Evangelism is what fundamentalists, evangelists, and evangelicals do. It is just not done now." Some find difficulty in believing and conceiving of evangelism outside the fundamentalist context.

The concept of faith-sharing is vital, regardless of how close the concept seems like the questing with proselytizing words from the fundamentalists. When the Christian churches abandoned this sharing in favor of keeping the traditions, they closed the social networks that reach out beyond church. Fewer and fewer church members talk about faith with family or friends.

The covid-19 epidemic has caused people in the world to close themselves off. Many church goers hold church online. Reaction to this deadly disease has caused some to resist the church altogether. The current response is unlike the plagues that struck the Roman Empire in 165 and 251. The flu epidemic of the 1917-1919 taught us something, but people are not prepared for the effects of this disease. The plague of 165 was probably smallpox. A third of the population died. The plague of 251 was measles and this pandemic caused another devastating result on the previously exposed population. Christians had a better explanation for these crises than the pagans. Christians were less afraid of death because of the promise of eternal life. Christians ministered to the sick. By living the faith, Christians provided a powerful example to non-believers of what being a Christian meant.

The phenomenal success came as they used social networks to attract people to the new faith. They evangelized their family members, friends, friends of friends, and acquaintances. They shared their faith wherever they traveled. Living God's vision of new life, they spread the joy to the vast Roman Empire.

Preaching was critical. I knew that and so I majored in the field of Preaching, Worship, and Literature at Vanderbilt. Preaching is used to apply the Christian faith to life situations. Preaching also addresses the new convert, the visitors, and the un-churched. Those with the gift of preaching help people unearth their joy, discover their human dignity. Good preaching in worship answers questions and helps listeners apply their Christian faith. The call to preach requires rigid training, study of the Holy Scriptures, the history of the church, pastoral counseling, biblical languages, archeology, education of children, youth and adults, and evangelism. Supervised field work and practical ministry experience.

Nothing is worse than dull sermons that drive people away and destroy the meaningfulness of service.

Ministers must have some introduction to music and singing. Music is a unique dimension of worship. My wife is director of music for Saint Paul United Methodist Church in Elmwood, Nebraska. We have a huge music room inside with vast pieces of music, a classy piano, a harp, bells, and a lifetime of experience. Her mother Bernice played organ and piano for 80 years before she died at age 92. Laurel will probably reach that zenith as she is herself now age 80. Her music is inspiring and deeply moving. Music touches souls and moves emotions. The choirs, hymns, and songs unite our voices, channel joy, and serves as a witness to beauty and elegance. It is power beyond words and human understanding. Music is key to an experience beyond our expression, to a joy beyond description, and moments of oneness that beaks the barriers of material living.

After I wrote *Spirit of Joy Church*, I then was inspired to write *The Joy of Prayer: The Way of Intimacy with God.* Prayer should be meaningful and inclusive to those present in worship. Some gifted ministers use times of silence to reinforce the intimacy with God. These periods permit practice in listening and private intercessions. Psalm 46:10 reminds us to "be still and know that I am God." Public worship makes the best impression if it captures the joy of Christian faith by projecting the presence of God, and inspiring confidence of God's involvement in the joys and struggles of living. When times are tough, joy can appear as impossible. In a world with a pandemic, we struggle just to smile, to pray, or drag ourselves out of bed. Despite the pains of living, we can learn to be content. How can we be content with millions dying of the Covid-19 disease? We must find opportunities to increase joy. Contentment comes with gratitude for our blessings. We can reflect on them each day. Focusing on gratitude increases satisfaction. Finding contentment is easier if we focus on the positive.

An old volume by H.R. Mackintosh, housed in the Yale University Library gave concrete examples for inspiring confidence including the conversation of Jesus with the Samaritan woman. Jesus' contact with this woman began with a simple need. "Give me a drink." John 4:7. He was natural and calm. His way was so different from how some begin in our day with "Are you saved? Or "Where will you spend eternity?" This woman wondered was his motivation or intention was for being so nice to a Samaritan. Jesus saw her need, a thirst for living water. Jesus said, "If you knew the gift of God, and who it was that is saying to you, 'Give me a drink,' you would have asked him, and he would have given you living water. John 4:10.

The woman's curiosity led to share more of herself. She said, "Sir, you have nothing to draw with, and the well is deep; where do you get that living water? Are you greater than our father Jacob, who gave us the well, and drank from it himself, and his sons, and his cattle?" John 4:11-12.

Jesus said, "Everyone who drinks of this water will thirst again, but whoever drinks of the water that I shall give him will never thirst again; the water that I give him will become in him a spring of water welling up into eternal life. John 4:13-14. This is the verse we printed on the bottles of cold water that was given to fans at the College World Series in Omaha.

This was her life need: perseverance and spiritual depth. She said, "Sir, give me this water." John 4:15. This story demonstrates the using of words in evangelism. (Mackintosh, H.R., *The Christian Experience of Forgiveness*. London: James Nisbet and Company, 1922, chapter 4, pp. 130-144.) A Spirit of Joy congregation embraces evangelism as fundamental to the reason they existence. Church growth is the natural result. Communicating faith is done in clear language without Christian traditional jargon that leaves out the unconverted. In leading the First Christian Church of Weeping Water, Nebraska, we organized 12 different small groups including an Alcoholics Anonymous group, a marriage enrichment group, an anger management group, an invincible seniors' group, a "lost and found" youth group, a prayer meeting group on Wednesday evenings before choir practice, a women's sewing group, and an early morning Saturday breakfast group. The small groups were designed to provide a chance for intimacy, a sense of belonging, and an opportunity to be oneself.

Joy oozes out as the church enthusiastically welcomes visitors and newcomers. The newly attracted are rapidly integrated into the life of the church. A church of joy gives a place that meets spiritual needs. They came because they found us welcoming and caring.

The phrase "love one another" occurs 13 times in John's letters. Here is where we find where love is so important. Love communicates our faith in Jesus to communities. Loving others is being obedient to God as we share it with others from our joy.

These letters are widely accepted as written by Jesus' beloved apostle who wrote the gospel of John. He wrote these letters while he lived in Ephesus. These short letters have the consistent theme of love. By exploring I John, readers understand the full deity and full humanity of Jesus Christ. Believers share a unity in lives full of joy as they share the love of Christ. II John gives encouragement to believers living faithfully. III John serves as a reminder for Christians to keep Christ at the center despite the divisions caused by struggles with sin. John explores the deep connection between obedience and love by showing how love for God is nothing without God's love for us. Humans can love because God first loved us. I John 4:19.

The apostle John talked, laughed, cried, and walked with Jesus. The love expressed in John's three letters is pertinent because we discover how to love like Jesus loved. Our joy becomes complete in Christ. His thoughts enable us to find out how to live like Jesus lived.

When we live in the "joy of the Lord," we can feel the bliss, the love, in a new awareness. When we feel disruption in ourselves or in the church community, we lose balance in our souls. With God's joy, Christians no longer exist in a black and white world. Life is then full of love with the rich colors in each area of living.

God's kingdom on earth and in heaven guides relationships, our calling for using gifts, and even how we view ourselves with *agape* love. Compassion replaces judging and holding on to grudges. Love opens people up for joy and miracles to happen.

The miracle involves a change from despair to being upbeat and positive, full of rushes and energy must like this writer feels now in composing this and other books for the glory of God. Love keeps from swimming in a pit of resentment, guilt, shame and inner turmoil. Love brings full freedom. Passion, empathy, and even romance comes like it has never been felt before. As a child going to Disneyland or some fun place, love sweeps in experiences of eternal love. Read I Peter 2:4-5.

John Wesley described the human situation as utterly destitute. The image of God is so distorted and disfigured that humankind can never redeem themselves. The self-induced slavery is so complete and so rooted in human nature. Love brings the incredible news that God has acted in the birth, life, death, and the resurrection of Jesus to make possible the redemption through the grace of God. (Eddie Fox, *Faith-Sharing*, p. 17)

Living the vision of God involves submission to the love of God. This fulfills the Great Commission. God is not only a seeking God. God is a sending God. Evangelism, conversion, and discipleship involve God is coming into the broken order of living to dwell with us.

Living in God's vision brings new insight, understanding, and changes in commitment. New life is born within. We are not the same. We see the world with new eyes. What was acceptable is now unacceptable. New commitments will bring the lure to guide us back to that older and less focused discipleship. Congregations must learn to discriminate among the world's attempts to gain attention. God is with us in all our genuine striving throughout the life journey on earth and life in the kingdom of heaven. Believers have nothing to fear and much to celebrate as God's beloved children. Agape love is not a natural endowment. We are not born with it. Like joy, nobody can conjure up love. The primary motive for evangelism comes from God, according to Michael Green, whose books are popular in the United Kingdom. Green observes, "The early Christians' motives were theological not institutional.

They shared faith because of the overwhelming experience of the love of God in Christ Jesus." (Michael Green, *Evangelism in the Early Church*, pp. 236-250.

Most ministers keep their jobs because they are part of the dominant culture. It is a safe way to be promoted to larger opportunities. One could spend his entire ministry without engaging with nondominant communities. Fitting in makes it easier to thrive and survive with engaging.

When one is in the nondominant culture, your extending grace to the dominant culture groups, you must have an unusual level of humility and grace. When one has lived within a nondominant cultural religious sphere, you become used to the dominant culture not needing you.

I have held the broken bodies of ministers suffering the pain. I have heard them cry out at the dominant churches who have never attempted to understand them.

In the vision quest to change, to learn, and to grow, those called or appointed to certain congregations will make mistakes privately and publicly. The believers who have accepted me as I am, have kept me from finding myself in such situations, because she alerts me ahead of time to the cultural land mines that I unknowingly step on. These culture tutors can see areas within any cultural context. They know intuitively that I might be keeping people out or discouraging them from being involved with me in the kingdom on earth. I have observed too many women and men who are tabbed as failures and choose to drop out. This is an ultimately critical time to have friends around you who love you enough to point out the potential for cultural misunderstandings and consequences. These vital folks can see with their own seasoned cultural lenses. They see things from their own experiences that you will never be able to spot on your own.

Willpower yields to "the strength of the joy of the Lord." We take care of body temples. We try to maintain a healthy weight. We are mindful of our physical hunger We might even hit our target weight ahead of schedule. We gain some assurance that our weaknesses are general human failings. We are in hock to biochemical processes that we cannot control. In a theology of conversion, we deal with free will. Free will is a notoriously difficult issue.

There is a difference between our acting freely on decisions made by ourselves. We are not forced to act against our human wills by someone or something outside. The paradox is that for us to be more in control, we must accept many things we will never control. Acceptance is the highest form of Christian faith. Free will is not about the ability to be right or wrong. It is about our ability to correct ourselves.

Humility in the conversion process is about accepting human limitations. What makes me humble as a preacher, teacher, and a writer is the genius of other people within my life circle.

Having and accepting human limitations gives assurance of being significant in the eyes of God. We are no less worthy in our weakened and fatigued realities. Our deepest reality is when we are deeply rooted in Christ Jesus. God offers unconditional love, mercy, and grace. These are the real treasures that shine like sparkling gems in the dark days. A single adult man felt his loneliness without a close friend in his circles. He prayed for wisdom and discernment to achieve a contented, more balanced life.

Most people spend most of life by themselves rather than in relationships. When living alone, I wrote many articles for *Christian Single Magazine*, published by the Sunday School Board of the Southern Baptist Convention. The apostle Paul and many mature believers today prefer living single. When we express honesty, most would sacrifice a part of their independence for the right life partner. Whether we live by ourselves or with others, we benefit from living a rich inner life.

To be converted into a richer inner life means that we process and experience emotionally, intellectually, gracefully, and beautifully the love of God. By professing and living with the inner Christ, those converted extend and deepen life by refection, memory, silent interrogation, and divine inspiration.

Several times each year, I engage with the monks in two Benedictine monasteries: Saint Benedict's Conference Center in Schuyler, Nebraska and Conception Abbey in Conception, Missouri. The monks in Missouri observe that "life begins at conception." It also begins at conversion.

My vision quests in both monasteries revealed that meals together are important parts of living in those communities. A monk said, "We do it with a communion aspect. This is an opportunity for service. It brings us together as a community. We can listen together as our meals are consumed in silence."

During special celebrations or in spiritual worship such as during seder meals, believers enjoy the communion gathering, they are together physically and spiritually. These simple spiritual times lead us into calmer minds and souls.

Dare to dream. You might be saying, "I'm too young." There is no such thing. Now is the time. God wants to use you. I was eight years old when I professed Christ as my Savior. By the time I was 12 years old, I had started preaching. Think about the young boy's lunch that Jesus used to feed 5,000 hungry people.

Others say, "I'm too old." Never stop envisioning. Use your wisdom and experience, your gifts and graces, if you can.

A new convert might say, "I'm too new to God." Look at Jesus' young disciples. Look at Paul. And they impacted the world. People say they are too tired, too insignificant, too encumbered by problems, or too hurt by people in and out of the church.

Margaret Clarkson had so many physical problems she knew she would never be a missionary. During her prayer time, she was reading John 20. She saw the words, "So send I you." God guided her to see where she lived was her mission field. She wrote this vision in a poem. She published the hymn, "So Send I You" in 1963. John Peterson composed the song. Peterson later shared the story of the writer of the poem which led her to a total commitment of her life to God. (Kenneth W. Osbeck, *Ibid.* pp. 83-85)

If the effectiveness of our evangelism is to be, God will help us unlock the power of vision. "And the Lord answered me, and said, write the vision and make it plain upon tables, that he may run that reads me." Habakkuk 2:2. People become excited when they hear this verse preached by a pastor. Some will shout. Some will give their neighbor a high five. Some with dance with enthusiasm.

It is sad to report that after hearing this powerful Word from God, many will not try or take time to write their vision. I have discovered that it takes more than just hearing a fresh inspirational message, reading a book, or attending a weekend retreat about envisioning. The key is to make a concentrated effort to take time to write out your vision. It requires an unwavering commitment to implement it. Read the book of Habakkuk several times. Vision is revealed to a believer in position to listen. To unlock the power of your vision, you must get alone with God to listen for God's guidance. Your vision must be written down in explicit details. Write your vision in plain, simple to understand language. This eliminates confusion that will hinder your progress. Envisioning will energize and ignite a fire of anticipation. This fire will motivate you to overcome life's discouragements, distractions, and disappointments that overcome the fact that living in the vision of God does not mean life is smooth sailing.

Frances Ridley Have gal was called "the consecration poet." At the age of four, she began reading and memorizing the entire Bible. By age seven, she was writing her thoughts in verse. She was sickly and frail, yet she was a rarely gifted student. She learned several modern languages as well as Hebrew and Greek. During her early adolescence, she had an emotional conversion experience. She said, "There and then I committed my soul to the Savior Jesus. Earth and heaven appeared so bright from that moment of joy." Frances was a natural musician. Churches and schools sought her to sing solos. She wanted to give her life to sing for Jesus. "Take My Life and Let It Be" was written by Miss Havergal in 1874.

She shared her story of effective evangelism. She tells of going on a visit for five days. Ten people were in the house. Some were not converted. The rest were not rejoicing Christians. God gave her a prayer: "Lord, give me all in this house." Before Frances left that house, everyone received a blessing of conversion. She said she was so filled with joy, she said she could not sleep and spent most of her last night in renewal of her consecration. She wrote that she was compelled to write words ending with "ever only, all for Thee." (Kenneth W. Osbeck, *Ibid.*, pp. 239-244)

Living the vision of God requires faith. Focusing on your vision helps faith grow. As we implement the vision, it will impact your life, your family, and those living in the kingdom of God. A Baptist director of missions reported on his evaluation sheet: "You are on target Jim. A lot of people talk about vision and desire to have a vision, but they do not spend the time seeking God for a vision. It is important to write your vision so that it is constantly before us. It is a reminder of the direction for our life."

A woman pastor in the United Methodist Church wrote, "I love what you say about making a vision plain. I think many times we just have this ethereal vision that is not concrete. And it really doesn't motivate us or give directions when the going gets tough."

The Bible is full of teachings concerning the importance of living with focused attention on Jesus. Living in God's vision enables us to seek values that hold eternal worth. Read Isaiah 45:22, Matthew 6:33, Hebrews 12:2, Colossians 3:1-3.

Helen Lemmel was given a tract entitled, "focused" in 1918. See read it, and focused on these words: "So then, turn your eyes upon Jesus, look full into his face and you will find the things of earth will acquire a strange dimness." She shared later, "Suddenly, as if commanded to stop and listen, I stood still, and singing in my soul and spirit, with not one conscious moment of putting word to word to create a rhyme, nor note to note to make a melody. The verses were written in the same week, after the usual manner of composition, but none less dictated by the Holy Spirit." She composed the hymn, "Turn Your Eyes Upon Jesus." (Kenneth W. Osbeck, 101 Hymn Stories, pp. 298-299)

How easy it becomes even for those of us who profess to be faithful followers of Jesus to get caught up with the "things of earth," so that our heavenly vision becomes blurred. Heaven is a place prepared for those who are prepared for it.

The preparation involves a search for meaning. That is like searching for a lost chord. When the lost chord is discovered, the discord of the world will be healed. The vision will be the symphony of earth coming into complete harmony. God is teaching us through our weaknesses and frailty to be obedient and dependent, to lean on the Lord's power. God wants to take the chronic disease, the pressure, the strain, and the stress from us. Read Isaiah 41:10.

Living in God's vision impresses us with the thought of God's grace, which is the unmerited favor of an omnipotent God in providing for our redemption. Living in grace causes us to realize with conviction, that it is grace and grace alone that assures us of an eternal relationship with God. There is nothing we can do or feel. Salvation is simply the personal appropriation of the wonderful grace of God. Grace gives us the courage to live the life of love. To postpone your dream and fear no more is to do at last what you came in the journey of life that you will love. God will awaken your spirit to adventure. Hold nothing back. Learn to find ease in risk. Our vision quest will continue if we live on earth.

When we peer into the darkened corridors of our souls, God's Light shines as it flares in our hearts and calls us home in the Next Place. We do not ignore the difficulties. Read Psalm 16:5-6. If you are blessed to have lived if I have, you have experienced sickness, physical limitations, bodily pains, and anxiety. Read Psalm 31:18. One day soon, we will instantly be in heaven because of the love of God. Ingratitude, comparison, greed, and constant complaining steals joy. Our vision quest is to be become real with ourselves and other people. As we closely abide with God, we are strengthened on the inside.

"The joy of the Lord is our strength."

"She was becoming sad. There is no joy involved in following others' expectations of yourself. "– Miriam Toews

Chapter Nine
Sharing the Joy with Spiritual Formation

Only when I began researching joy at Vanderbilt did I come upon the term "spiritual formation." Many ministers and churches viewed spiritual formation as heretical and new age. Spiritual formation is widely accepted today in most churches. It is now taught as a separate class in theological seminaries. Spiritual formation is shaped and directed by the context where it happens. The native environment is in the fellowship of believers, the gathered community of Christians, the church. Throughout church history, the community has provided a royal priesthood of women and men who have shared "the whole counsel of God."

Spiritual formation is the green twig on the venerable bough in the Kingdom of Joy. The dynamic Christian love is unquestionably expressed in the early church. John Chrysostom was preacher and pastor during the age of the Church Fathers. He tried to modify the humiliating practice of public penance as a requirement to be admitted to communion. In his writing his *Treatise on the Priesthood*, he put a light on the teaching that "no one can, by compulsion, cure an unwilling person. "Chrysostom said he was anointed to be a physician of the soul. The word "psychotherapy" comes from two New Testament Greek words that mean "healing of the soul."

Be patient with yourself and stop expecting miracles. God sees us as unique, special, and important. In spiritual formation we learn to not let the opinions of others shape how we view ourselves. Be proud of who you are. Allow the joy of accepting you just as you are to overshadow everything else.

In this book, I want to suggest some approaches that places spiritual formation in the context of evangelism and discipleship. Evangelism, as well as much of my writing on mental health, prayer, sexuality, the Spirit of Joy, the origin of Baptists and other sects and denominations, and my view of the resurrection of Jesus and the next life has not been popular, but necessary and pertinent.

Without discussing of these vital topics, a Good News account, a loving and relational God, an incarnational Christ, and a guiding Holy Spirit, there is no spiritual formation. The response has always been a decision to follow Christ, which is marked by repentance, baptism, and being together with other believers. When a person decides to follow Jesus and then affiliates with a particular faith environment, discipleship begins. Discipleship means learning concrete behaviors. Character and ethics matter. Part of is learning the historical and theological foundations of the gathered church. Spiritual practices such as prayer, worship, engagement in social concerns, and the sacraments. Christian discipleship is contextualized in a particular place with particular people holding ideas and promoting teachings. There is a critical need to promote spiritual formation to bring about genuine life changes in the church. Spiritual formation is the process of shaping our spirit. This shaping is done by the Holy Spirit. Spiritual formation in Christ is the process of imitating the qualities and character of Jesus.

Consolidating the differing usages and nuances of spiritual formation is an enormous task to include biblical and theological insights. It also includes multidisciplinary knowledge in psychology, education, history, and philosophy.

J. P. Palmer's discussion of what shapes spiritual formation includes the practice of prayer, study of the scriptures, and the gathered life of the community. Palmer believes that Christians are formed spiritually through his three areas of concern within a Christian environment. Palmer views spiritual formation as the same as discipleship but expressed in the term that relates better with some today. His concept of spiritual formation is the direct action of the Spirit upon the inner person. Palmer's definition cuts across denominational lines and historical traditions with the call for believers to return to the basic of becoming like Christ.

Spurgeon said of prayer, "Prayers are heard in heaven very much in proportion to our faith. Little faith will get great mercies, but great faith still greater."

Throughout Christian history, devout believers have recognized the necessity of maintaining intimate relations with God through the channels of prayer.

Prayer is as basic to spiritual formation as breathing is to our natural lives. Prayer exhaling the spirit of humankind and inhaling the Spirit of God. Prayer is an attitude for life. Whenever we spend time with God, prayer becomes a sweet and meaningful hour in our lives.

Spiritual formation has come to me as the way to deeper life in Christ. Spiritual formation is the process of being conformed to the image of Christ for the glory of God and for the sake of the world. Read II Corinthians 3:17-18. The Spirit guides the ongoing journey. The Spirit and the written Word, and the in-dwelling Christ is "living water" flowing out of the innermost being, coming from the deepest depths of souls and transformed communities. Spiritual discipline means doing concrete habits which caused full attention to grace. Submission to the Spirit, space or solitude, reflection, accountability, and humility of the mind and heart. As the stated vision of creating an atmosphere where joy and miracles happen. Doing the vision in the churches where I have served involved a stable platform of theology, ethics, and faithful relationship practices engaging in the concerns of the world as did Christ.

Spiritual formation, as I discussed in the chapter, "A Historical View of Conversion," the history of the church traces the term to Roman Catholic doctrine. Unknown in Protestant circles for hundreds of years, today, it is a popular title in publications, sermons, and in revival type quests for the joy of salvation. Part of postgraduate level programs have reinforced the value of spiritual formation to the body of Christ. In the spiritual growth journey of believers, different concepts and definitions have been shared. Spiritual formation is a restoration to spiritual discipline practices in the early church desert fathers and Jesus' disciples. **A Theology of Spiritual Formation**

When I wrote *Dancing with God: A Theology of Joy*, published in 2016, Deliberately used the title "a theology," not "the theology." Most of the books that I consulted discussed the need for biblical and theological support for spiritual formation to prevent it from becoming just another fad that never gets entrenched into the Body of Christ. That is the essence of what the apostle Paul suggests in II Corinthians. Read II Corinthians 3:18. In this passage of scripture Paul describes what we call spiritual formation with how believers are transformed into the likeness of Christ. He sees this process as for a lifetime. He views the Holy Spirit in the conversion of souls as God's glory is restored when believers are transformed. As believers become transformed into the image of God, the covenant community of believers will display God's image to the world where humanity will know the glory of God.

A theology of spiritual formation would not be complete without including the two greatest commandments in Mark 12:29-31. These two commandments show the outcomes for spiritual formation as a human person is more like Jesus. The first greatest commandment comes from the Shema of Judaism where it is the Jewish creed of spiritual formation.

That declaration of "the Lord is one" in Mark 2:29 reveals monotheism and the recognition of wholeness or the oneness of God. Worshippers of God must have the same wholeness or oneness of integrity when they come before God. They are enabled to come before God with integrity of heart, soul, mind, and strength as required in the first commandment from Christ.

The second commandment is required of believers to love their neighbors as themselves. Healthy neighborly love is knowing how to love themselves. Spiritual formation is an outgoing process where believers learn and develop right relationships with God, self, and others. As believers live in Christ, they attain the goals of spiritual formation as a natural part of their lives. Spiritual formation is not a way for one to earn salvation. It is the work of the Holy Spirit after salvation for believers to conform and develop into Christ's image and likeness.

The core center of biblical theology is the establishment of the people of God. Two Bible stories, God's deliverance of the Israelites from Egypt in Exodus 6:7, and Paul's concept of the temple of the Holy Spirit in I Corinthians 3:16-17. God gave the Ten Commandments to help a group of slaves to become the people of God.

The Bible provides the content and source for spiritual formation to happen. Paul highlighted the importance of scripture for spirituality in II Timothy 3:16. The Bible is not just a description of what happened in the past, but it gives direction for how we live now. The Word is Jesus giving the models that are biblical and appropriate. Spiritual formation brings awareness into the living as they take time for conversations and reflection of the encounters faced on the journey. New and clearer glimpses of the story of God are found in the stories of our sisters and brothers.

A Spirit of Joy gathering is intended to be the fertile soil in which spiritual life is born, blossoms, and bears fruit. This is the place anointed by Christ for supporting the spiritual journey. The church is where people learn how to follow Christ. As our lives are transformed, we are given the grace and wisdom to become guides to others as they seek to walk with God. In our gathering in the presence of God, we get to know each other at greater depth.

Our appreciation for each other grows. Here we find encouragement to discover full reconciliation and closer community.

Beginning in first grade, I was fascinated with girls. Getting to know women brought a mystery and joy and depth. If I could make a young lady laugh, I thought I saw the most beautiful thing on earth. My mother was but a teenager when I was born. People would kid me and say, "Is she your girlfriend?"

God created women and men for companionship. God wants to relate with us. Spiritual formation is the way in which we become aware of God's companionship. Spiritual formation must do not only with our souls but with God. We cannot predict where and when God will break into our lives. No one structure of spiritual formation and no definition can contain the reality. Read Ephesians 3:16-17. Only God can make God known to us. The Holy Spirit cannot be bound. God walks with us in ways we are not aware of, beyond human expectations. We practice the disciplines and seek models, new paradigms, methods, to open us to God's self-disclosure. Our experiences with God will never end in our vision quests.

The word "Comforter" as applied to the Holy Spirit would be better translated by a more vigorous word like strength. Jesus' words are not for the faint-hearted. It is a blood transfusion for the soul. Mother Teresa said, "The highest joy that can be known by those who rely on the Spirit comes in mysterious ways."

We go through the life journey as a transient on our way to eternity in the Next Place. We were created in God's image. With that image debased, we need to be taught how to meditate, to practice intimate prayer, and tools to guide us in the relationship with God.

Spiritual disciplines continue the conversion process as we explore our inner most depths. Read Psalm 42:7. They create time and space for transformation. Disciplines are training exercises for living a life in the image of God. It is wise to choose to do them regularly.

Expecting external results without inner transformation is soul-killing and not life-giving. As a result of the Reformation, confessionals were abandoned as a church sacrament. The church rediscovered itself as a congregation of representatives of Christ in the teaching of "the priesthood of all believers," giving every Christian a duty and a right to spiritual formation.

During the age of the Puritans in England, society changed radically. The church offered guidance in making moral decisions. Public preaching and teaching were followed by visitation in their home or in the priest's home.

There is no formulized definition for spiritual formation in the history and entities in the Christian world. Some propagate their personal preferred definitions. These people consider other definitions as inadequate. Church leaders will find difficulty finding clarity with the many definitions that are used. Pastors and other church leaders can determine the appropriate and biblically supported definition for their local church. William Willimon, a bishop of the United Methodist Church, challenged the Methodist tradition that "all answers flow from the top down," and that has been "killing us." Today, a Christian who is looking for a church home, they first visit a local congregation. If there is a visionary pastor, if the Holy Spirit appears to be active in the life of the congregation, and if there is joy and engaging worship, they will visit again. If not, they attend someplace else, regardless of the denominational label on the front sign. (William Willimon and Andy Langford, *A New Connection: Reforming the United Methodist Church*, p.38.)

The congregation gathered to worship and serve God is the font from which flows Christian good to receive, nurture, equip, and send disciples of Jesus Christ. Willimon writes, "The local congregation is not a branch office for the national denomination, not a franchise outlet for denomination programs." (*Ibid.*, pp. 41-74) Willimon spent a lot of "writing energy" writing in his book on the local church.

This author spent an hour at breakfast at the Lake Junaluska Conference Center in North Carolina discussing how we both felt called and gifted to serve the whole ecumenical church. His sermons from the beautiful Memorial Chapel at Duke University reflected his passion for the church's mission. Willimon is gifted and continues to write for Abingdon, the publishing arm of the United Methodist denomination, in his retirement years. He knows John Killinger, my mentor, and speaks in many denominations' conferences and assemblies in which he reflects my own vision of joy. Passive believers who are satisfied with their salvation and status have low desire to seek inner transformation within them.

Pastors who have the gifts and graces can lead their local congregations into an atmosphere change will experience the joy of seeing not only mere numbers coming to worship, but authentic transformation and maturity.

Bishop William Willimon writes of his feeling that there was something dead wrong with how local churches do ministry and their long-range planning. He does not view the current situation as reflecting the guidance of God. It is what Christ thinks should be done. There is nothing more pathetic than a church without the joy of prayer and Bible study was expressed by an Alaskan pastor, who asked, "What would it mean for the church to move out into the deeper water and cast our nets into sea of the world?" (William Willimon, *A New Connection: Reforming the United Methodist Church*, pp. 46-49.)

Discipleship on what has been termed the right wing of the church means preparation for soul winning. Right wingers often farm out this area to parachurch ministries because even they do not want to the work themselves. The left wing, including the mainline congregations, use a social activity, serving in food ministries, blood banks, and political protest as expressions of evangelism. Praying in color is a fresh concept created by Sybil Macbeth. Praying in color uses pens, crayons, or markers rather than just words and silence. The concept is a fresh new way to practice the Great Commission. Praying in color can re-energize the prayer lives of kingdom people. The apostle Peter tells us spiritual formation adds virtue to our faith, knowledge to the virtue, self-control to our knowledge, patience to our self-control, godliness to our patience, brotherly kindness to our godliness, and divine love to brotherly kindness. II Peter 1:5-7. Peter assures us that the eternal kingdom of God will be provided for us a long time before we leave our earthly journey to live in the next place.

Let joy keep you. Reach out your hands and take it.

"Our responsibility is to preach and teach Christ's dynamic Gospel. It is the Holy Spirit's responsibility to make our witness effective." --Bill Bright

Chapter Ten
NEW VISION WITH CREATIVE PASSION

As minister of joy to the world, I find joy every day. I have had many opportunities and possibilities from my birth. My mother prayed for me giving her first-born son her love and adoration. She visualized my being called as a preacher. As a child, I thought I might be an evangelist. My home church had four revivals almost every year. I got a front seat to hear God's work and to witness conversions and baptisms. I continue to believe that God offers salvation. Revivals are not held often. Any "protracted meetings" are now weekend retreats or one day with somebody preaching, but hardly ever a conversion. I do not call myself an evangelist and I call my revivals Joyquests or Visionquests for Joy. The church of today has lost its ability to lead people in the conversion process. Doing it in the same way as we did in the past will lead to more spiritual disasters. In today's culture few churches think and decide to attempt something new. Few attempt a two-week revival. Most try a three-or-four-day revival, and even if they get a well-known preacher, few show up.

Churches must have leaders with competency and the ability to create a roadmap for implemented effective evangelism, conversion, and spiritual formation. The grace of God is not about earning. It is concerned about action. God has given a way to "work out" our salvation "with fear and trembling. "The joy of salvation saturates believers with a calm assurance that it is God who is at work in us to complete what God has accomplished with love. Read Philippians 2:12-13.

The Great Commission requires us to "comfort ye, comfort ye" those who visit our congregation, then they will be nurtured and inspired to return. In the churches where the welcome is cold, demanding, exclusive, or overbearing, they will not sense God's presence. Creating an atmosphere where joy and miracles happen will invite the Spirit. This environment will honor every person's unique gifts. The faithful response to God will give permission for the transforming vision of God to happen in the lives of all. God's Spirit is always present. The psalmist declared that it is impossible to escape that presence. Read Psalm 139:7-12.

My purpose in writing this book is to analyze the problem. And to offer some insights into what individuals and their congregations can conceive. More work and courage are needed. God may be calling some young person to just do it.

Today, the world needs new evangelizers. That is the purpose for this book. I pray that readers develop a deeper appreciation of our abundant lives in Jesus Christ and the treasure of Christian faith.

The world would be black as pitch and our souls equally dark without God's forgiveness and mercy, and the joy of discovering the light. What a privilege, what a gift! May we aim and live a life that pleases God above all things. Living in the kingdom of joy opens us to see God in others and honor the footprint in their souls. Jesus is ours for eternity.

Every day we meet other people. In a year, we touch thousands of people. Each person is a conduit of God's living in our world.

Paul Few, the director of the men's ministry of the Nebraska Region of the Christian Church (Disciples of Christ) reminded me of his joy that the most attended Men's February Retreat at the First Christian Church of Nebraska City was when I shared my vision for a new concept of understanding evangelism, discipleship and conversion in the future church. My session themes for that Saturday workshop were in alliteration words: Joy Inauguration, Joy Information, Joy Imagination, and Joy Inspiration.

In Joy Inauguration, I reminded the men that no vision is meaningful until it happens. The joy of the Lord is implemented when people in the community are willing to respond to the call to create a Spirit of Joy in the churches represented by the men gathered.

In Joy Information, I gave some of my concepts of joy gathered over 50 years. Continuing education is a hallmark of the contemporary church. The annual retreat broadens the range of options in the changing world. Because of today's technology, the distance between us has been eliminated giving new opportunities to connect with one another.

In Joy Imagination, the men enjoyed visualizing the Spirits leading to realize what will come to pass, to see what is possible. Imagination shapes a dream and reveals the possibilities by showing disciples the difference that a life filled with joy makes in our own lives and in the lives of others.

In joy's inspiration, we saw joy as a fruit of the Spirit, a gift from God. As participants shared their own journeys of where each experienced joy, we doubled our personal joy in our memories said to be the highlight of the vision quest for joy. My credentials for writing this book include my calling as a communicator. in my call and my gifts and graces, journalism, preaching and teaching, and counseling.

Some of my fellow Christians scorn at my work with a doctoral degree in psychology and a licensed mental health practitioner. There are quite a few psychologists and psychiatrists who professed the Christian faith. They contribute as an influential presence in clinical circles. A mental health practitioner who is a Christian uses theoretical and practical insights from many sources. The field of psychology is a divided field. Denominational leaders are so fascinated with psychology and rely solely on psychological teachings and practices that that omit the realities in spiritual formation. Eddie Fox gave an emotional appeal at several annual conference meetings that the Methodists need to require a study in evangelism as well as clinical pastoral education in preparation for ordination.

Conversion and spiritual formation of the inner self into the character of Christ cannot be achieved without the life of God living in the soul. Considering the Great Commission, a life of spiritual formation is indispensable. Knowing Christ with extensive prayer, solitude and silence will create a disciple whose "joy be complete." John 16:24.

I seek to focus on my soul's longing for joy and to encourage joy to flourish. Joy does not appear when we try to hold it all together. The "joy of the Lord" comes when you allow God to hold you. **"Everything became now. My horses, cows, and hogs and even everybody changed." –A converted Nebraska farmer.** Chapter Eleven**Warming People with Passionate Fire**

Warming God's children with passionate fire is a way to describe my life journey as the Minister of Joy to the World. Passionate evangelism is like fire.

Like fire, I gain energy from the moments of joy as I fan the fire and I consume it.
Like fire, I generate heat and light.
Like fire, I expand freely in all directions.
Like fire, I dance with God in the air.
Like fire, I ascend to the heavens.
Like fire, I burn with hunger for more life.
Like fire, I am deeply involved in my experiences.
Like fire, I leave nothing behind me.
Like fire, I am filled with creative passion.
Like fire, I consume all obstacles and use them for fuel.
Like fire, I inspire people with my intensity.
Like fire, I warm people with my passionate joy.

Visionquests for Joy International is the fire we share. God has blessed us to be enabled to share the Great Commission. Our fires burn as brightly as the fires of revival. The Spirit of Joy has brought many mainline and other congregations to discover new passion for evangelism.

An effective vision quest is more than a strategy, more than a method. God uses our passion that crystallizes in a life of joy. What do the churches lack? Most congregations have enough money, time, and structure. Fervent love for God with a creative passion is the secret for effective evangelism. The flame of fire must be fanned with enthusiasm to consume all obstacles. Barriers to the spread of the gospel must be identified and used as fuel. The sparks of faith will not be ignited. A fire must spread to stay alive. Firefighters in California and the west know this better than anybody.

The beginning of the Great Commission was the fire resting on each believer. This event brought the gift of the Holy Spirit which enabled them to speak intelligibly in other languages. This miracle brought representatives of different nationalities and ethnic groups into the kingdom of joy. Now the commission extends in widening circles from Jerusalem, to Judea, to Samaria and eventually to every nation and territory. The fire of the Holy Spirit is an eternal flame that will never be extinguished.

Christians are called to use their gifts and graces to attract lost people to the joy of salvation. There is a host of seminary graduates who are up to date, intellectual and theological. I often ask if their approach is adequate for the challenge of this hour. They preach and teach the subjects that are popular in the moment. We must recover communication from the pulpits considering eternity as well as the kingdom of God now. We must recognize the missing piece, "the e-word," evangelism. We are called by Christ to enlist voluntarily in evangelistic proclamation.

God in infinite mercy poured out the Spirit when the church was born. God can do the same miracles at the culmination of its history. We need the fire of God to ignite a spiritual force to overcome the apathy. God has lit the wick. The language of Zion is not spoken with clarity by women and men who are responsible. The silence of the church against the things that concern God puts the church asleep. The pillars of the church have been converted into pillows. Spiritual formation is a priority, but the church is lukewarm because the members of the church are not on fire. Read Acts 1:8.

My purpose for writing this book is to examine why churches, influenced bypast conversion theology and practices. The urgency of being able to identify the underlying problems cannot be overstated. Every fiber in the church to bear witness to the joy of salvation needs to be examined and tested. Lamentations 3:40. One reason we are not effective is that we make fallacious assumptions about the people God is wanting to reach. These challenges require finding new ways of communicating the gospel clearly in a new context characterized by difference and dissolution. By dissolution, I mean the end of basic assumptions about the definition of words such as God, love, joy, salvation, conversion, and evangelism. A gap emerges between the witnesses and those who hear the message. The church needs to reexamine how to carry out its mission in this new world.

Eddie Martin, an itinerant Southern Baptist evangelist, who in the 1950's held big tent revivals in Bristol, Virginia used to say, "We illuminate ourselves with the dying glow of our own light, rather than in the lory of Christ."

Christians are the architects of their own ineffective weakness. I gain energy like a fire as I set spiritual fires for God as I share "the joy of the Lord." The fire inside us burns forever. I feel as young today as I feel the warmth of my soul. This eternally youthful life is like the joy of the sea coming home to the shore.

During the hot Nebraska summer days, I walk around the neighborhood. I enjoy seeing the acres of corn and soybeans that cover the land. I gather some fallen branches, some dried up leaves from the fall. I grab a scrap piece of paper from the recycling bin. I light a small spark to the low edges of the crumpled paper. I watch he fire climb. On this lovely summer night which becomes dim after nine o'clock with daylight time, the fire gently pulls itself up the sides of the paper and moves to the dry leaves and grasses.

As the fire slowly grows, I feel the warmth in my face and throughout my body. The sky turns from its dimmed, late evening blue to dancing colors of a Nebraska sunset: baby skinned pink, hot reds and oranges, purple, and unnamed hues. Somewhere between the beauty of the night and the fire crackling just beyond my feet, there is a fullness that catches my breath, inviting me to listen, to remember that I am not in this joy alone.

As I stare into the tiny fire, I notice the fire moving from within the pit. The flames are dancing like the ones in my artificial living room fireplace. The gentle shifting of the fire responds to the summer breeze. The wisps and puffs of smoke tail toward our neighbor's lawn and then shift toward a corn field. Just a small wind coaxes the fire to move in a new direction. Suddenly, the whole fire stands still. I wondered if I should put more tree branches or dry leaves into the dying embers. The fire continued to move, stretching upward as if it was waking from a refreshing nap. The fire now has a renewed energy.

I begin to breath more deeply. Then like the fire, I stand silent. The quiet is like the fire when it has consumed the kindling, the broken branches, and the dry leaves. It turns toward the bigger logs, the main course. Evangelism involves a spiritual fire that invites those around it to know and follow Christ.

I am reminded of the spiritual song by Kurt Kaiser called "Pass It On." The song was a breakthrough in Southern Baptist worship. In my mind's joy video, I can still hear the people at Ridgecrest Baptist Conference Center in North Carolina sing, "It only takes a spark to get a fire going, and soon those all around can warm up in its glowing; that's how it is with God's love, once you've experienced it: you spread God's love to everyone, you want to pass it on. ("Kurt Kaiser "Pass It On," *Chalice Hymnal*, number 477)

We are too embarrassed to invite people to worship with us unless we have something attractive to entice them. Back in Nebraska I turn over the remaining pieces of the charred log. Gathering the ashes from the middle of the fire pit, I wonder if a vision of spreading a cultureless gospel would be possible. Doing evangelism is not to be determined by the cultural context, as if the cultural context is a firm foundation to build effective evangelism. No matter the desire to avoid passing on the distortions and deformities from the culture. The gospel is nothing if it cannot grow new life in every culture through which it is preached.

The last embers from the fire cracks pulling my attention back. I stare at the hot place where the fire was flaming. My thoughts drift back toward evangelism. God chose to incarnate and embody the gospel in a Hebrew culture. Next, God lit the flame of the gospel within the Greco-Roman culture, and in a host of cultures since then.

The night sky is darker. A few clouds moved in and blocked some of the stars that were seen earlier. The fire is burning low. I debate building another fire, but I decide it is now too late. With my warm bed in mind, I return to the fire to pour water on what remains. Smoke and steam rise upward only to be moved along by the wind. I walk back inside and continue writing on my vision of how the church can envision the Great Commission.

Confusion in the Struggle with Evangelism

Thank you for reading this book. The appalling environment for doing the Great Commission will not change unless Christian believers become aware. We can be part of the solution. We can help build the kingdom of God. When your soul is kindled, and you step out onto fresh ground, you will be young again with new energy. May my thoughts in this book unfurl you into the grace of beginning.

In my decades of experience, I have never felt such confusion and fear. This confusion has opened the door to the plundering of evangelism. We need to create a new wine skin as Jesus told us. Mark 2:22.

If we continue to be out of sync and confused, evangelism will struggle to get traction. Having gentle conversations with our fellow strugglers is based on joy not on fear. The kingdom of God is built on "the joy of the Lord." The goal of the church is to evangelize the world. The priority of the kingdom people

is to ensure that every person in the world hears and understands the words of the gospel. We must share the Good News with joy and grace and love.

The Great Commission includes the going, the proclamation, the baptism after the profession of faith, and the discipleship of believers. The motive for evangelism is to glorify God. As a believing Christian is being explained to a non-believer, Jesus Christ is esteemed, honored, and glorified because the gospel in about Jesus. Read Habakkuk 2:14 and I Corinthians 10:31.

Each Christian's calling is to do all things for God's glory, not our own. Bringing the joy of the Lord causes our efforts to be fruitful and we experience the joy of the conversions of souls.

Witness is a legal term. If we are witnessing for Christ, it is like being a witness in a courtroom. We explain the facts of Jesus' life and the significance of those facts for salvation. Witness also means to tell our testimony. We share the difference Christ has made in our lives. We see a host of examples in the book of Acts. Witnessing and evangelizing are the same thing.

To free those under their care, leaders must share the joy of obedience. Albert Schweitzer taught, "Example is not the main thing in influencing others. It is the only thing." People in the church will be further confused as they think that if evangelism is so important, why do not our leaders do it. With renewed understanding, church leaders will be fizzing with joy about their evangelism encounters. They will share in their sermons as well in casual conversations. Joy is the key term as we discover the excitement in new wine skins.

Jesus is the pastor of our pastors. His priority is to know how we are progressing with the Great Commission. I pray that this book will be a gift for you. Read Paul's appreciation of the beautiful feet of those who bring the gospel to a world starved for love in Romans 10:14-15.

God has chosen each one of us to live in our earthly journey during these years and not any other time. God knew that in this time in history was the right moment for us. Everything about it would enable us to do what only we can do. It is the time for us, and we are for this time. We came in this time in history because God has a calling to use all we are to enable God's beloved to experience grace in abundance. God chose us to be ambassadors to bring love to this moment in human history.

The love of God allows for understanding our place. When we are understood, we nourish the joy of being loved. John 3:16. When this joy dawns upon you, you feel the freedom to release yourself into the will of God. When love awakens in your life it is like a Nebraska dawn breaking within you. Where before there was anonymity, now there is an intimacy. Where before there was fear, now there is courage. Where before there was an awkwardness in sharing your surprises of joy, now there is grace. I pray this book will awaken you as a new beginning.

We need to step boldly into the culture of this day and fulfill the commission. Before we can preach the gospel, we must know what the gospel is. There are many false ideas in the marketplace of today's culture. I was born in 1942 during the second world war. **Turbulent Times**

After the war, there came a time of self-discovery, and the time was unique to any other time. The culture was changing quickly. Some became new believers. As the decades rapidly passed, humans became fascinated with new technology, humanism, and the masses were stirred by the new culture. These ideas created a heavy force that sought an open and free ethic that indulged the appetite that pushed aside the eternal ways of God. "If it feels good, do it" was the theme. Add into the mix consciousness-altering drugs humans created an atmosphere for new problems. The Word of God was drowned out by these voices. Paul's letter to the Ephesians speaks to our time. Read Ephesians 1:4.

Turbulent times brought heavy questions like who am I and why am I? The world could have avoided much suffering, sin, and senseless wars within and without if the will of God had been sought by this generation. They would have discovered that belief in Jesus brought true peace and freedom, love, and joy. Disillusioned and filled with the bewitching notion of humans as the center enchanted them as seductively as it had Adam and Eve.

The tenor of our time makes our call in the Great Commission more urgent than ever. We must share our faith now in the circumstances of the twenty-first century. To become evangelizers of Jesus through the witness of our lives, we consider several questions. Who is Jesus Christ to me? Do I reflect Christ's presence? Do I evaluate life's events from a faith perspective? These questions help us to determine areas where we need progress. The answers can inspire us to move forward in the kingdom. I want to drain the last ounce of joy.

In our old or newly created messages for evangelization, we must proclaim what Jesus wants to communicate to our world. This proclamation of faith is the *kerygma* in Greek. The word means preaching. The apostle Paul told us this is the usual way to communicate. Romans 10:17. Paul anticipated our turbulent times. See II Timothy 4:5. The time is now.

We are expected to evangelize. Each time we pray, we can ask for people to come into our path throughout the day to share our faith. Read I Peter 3:15. We can be ready by simply sharing our own testimony of the actions of God in our lives. We can tell three things: how we were before we knew Jesus, what happened when we got to know Jesus, and how we are now. In my many years of doing evangelism, I have discovered that a personal testimony remains the most effective way to fulfill the Great Commission. With the power of the Holy Spirit in us, we imbue today's culture with the gospel. We are to be used to transform the world.

For those new to sharing your testimony, you will find joy in being the first ripple to make an impact in the sea of contemporary culture. "The joy of the Lord is our strength," as we are given "every spiritual blessing in the heavenly places. "Ephesians 1:3.

As I close this book, and readers finish the reading, will you promise to make use of the strategies shared. Focus on Jesus and the will of God. Pray that your witness will bring grace, love, and joy. Francis of Assisi said, "Preach the gospel, and use words when necessary."

We do not have to go back to the "good old days." We must bloom where we are planted. We are being called to go inwardly to be taught and converted by the Holy Spirit. Most of us struggle with silence. We cannot wait to speak out. We feel we must challenge the world with God's radical message. Without the Spirit dwelling inside, there would never be an eternal change or transformation. The transformation redeems each moment for all ages and years for all eternity.

Be ready for excitement, surprising joy, and a great adventure as we take faith and "pass it on."

Bibliography

Althaus, Paul. *The Theology of Martin Luther*. Philadelphia: Fortress, 1966.Anderson, Ray. *Ministry on the Fireline*. Downers Grove: InterVarsity Press, 1983.Andrews Edward. *The Kingdom Life: A Practical Theology of Discipleship and*

Spiritual Formation. Colorado Springs: NavPress, 2010.Armstrong, K.A. *A History of God: The 4000-Year Quest of Judaism, Christianity, and Islam*. New York: Ballantine Books, 1993.Averbeck, Robert E. "Spirit, Community, and Mission: A Biblical Theology for

Spiritual Formation, *Journal of Spiritual Formation and Soul Care*, I, pp. 27-53.

Banister, Doug. *The Word and Power Church*. Grand Rapids: Zondervan, 1999.Barreiro, Alvaro. *Basic Ecclesial Communities: The Evangelization of the Poor*.

Maryknoll, New York: Orbis, 1982.Brauer, Jerald. "Conversion: From Puritanism to Revivalism," *The Journal of Religion*. 58, no.3, July 1978: pp. 227-243.

Beazley, Hamilton and Claude E, Payne. *Reclaiming the Great Commission*. San Francisco: Jossey-Bass, 2002.Beckman, William A. *Redefining Revival: Biblical Patterns for Mission, Evangelism, and Church Growth*. Houston: Touch Publications, 2004.

Biederwolf, William E. *Evangelism: Its Justification, Its Operation and Its Value*. New York: Revell, 1921.

Boursier, Helen T. *Tell It with Style: Evangelism for Every Personality Type*. Downers Grove: InterVarsity Press.

Bonhoeffer, Dietrich. *Life Together*. New York: Harper and Row, 1954.

Bonhoeffer, Dietrich. *The Cost of Discipleship*. New York: Harper and Row, 1956.

Brekus, Catherine A. *Strangers and Pilgrims: Female Preaching in America, 1740-1845*. Chapel Hill, North Carolina: University of North Carolina Press, 1998.

Brown, Lester. *Outgrowing the Earth: The Food Security Challenge in an Age of Falling Water Tables and Rising Temperatures*. New York: Norton, 204.

Bryan, Dawson Charles. *A Handbook of Evangelism for Laymen*. Nashville: Abingdon-Cokesbury, 1948.

Buddle, Michael and Robert Brimelow, eds. *The Church as Counterculture*. Albany, New York: State University of New York, 2000

Bunch, Cindy. *Small Group Idea Book; Resources for Enriching Evangelism*. Downers Grove: InterVarsity Press, 1999.

Bushnell, Horace. *Christian Nurture*. New York: Charles Scribner's Sons, 1923.

Burne, Mary. Trans. "Be Thou My Vision," *Chalice Hymnal*, hymn number 495. Saint Louis: Chalice Press, 1995.

Chapman, Gary. *The Five Love Languages*. Chicago: Northfield Publishing Company, 2010.

Clapp, Rodney. *A Peculiar People: The Church ss Culture in a Post-Christian Society*. Downers Grove: InterVarsity Press, 1999.

Clouse, Robert G, Richard Peirard, and Edwin M. Yamaunchi. *The Two Kingdoms: The Church and Culture Through the Ages of Church History*. Chicago: Moody Press, 1994.

Dean, Jeremy. *Making Habits: Why We Do Things, Why We Do not, and How to Make Any Change Stick*. Boston: De Capo Press, 2014.

Dean, Kenda. Almost Christian: *What the Faith of Our Teenagers Is Telling the American Church*. Oxford: Oxford University Press, 2010.

Dickson, John. *The Best Kept Secret of Evangelism and Christian Mission*. Grand Rapids: Zondervan, 2012.

Donoghue, Emma. *The Pull of the Stars: A Novel*. London: Little, Brown, and Company, 2020

Finney, Charles. *Lectures on Revivals of Religion.* Cambridge: Harvard University Press, 1970.

Foster, R.T. *Celebration of Discipline: The Path to Spiritual Growth.* London: Hodder and Stoughton, 1989.

Fox, Eddie and George Morris. *Faith-Sharing.* Nashville: Discipleship Resources, 2000 edition.

Fredeickson, B.L. *The Oxford Companion to Emotion and the Affective Sciences.* New York: Oxford University Press, 2009.

Gaventa, Beverly. *From Darkness to Light: Aspects of Conversion in the New Testament.* Philadelphia: Fortress Press, 1986.Gladden, Washington. *The Christian Pastor.* New York: Charles Scribner's Sons, 1923

Green, Michael. *Evangelism in the Early Church.* Grand Rapids: Eerdmans, 2003.

Haacker, Klaus. *The Theology of Paul's Letter to the Romans.* Cambridge: Cambridge University Press, 2003.

Haikkinen, Jacob. "*Notes on Epistrepho and Matanoeo,*" Ecumenical Review 19, no. 3, July 1967, pp. 313-318.

Hankins, Barry. *The Second Great Awakening and the Transcendentalists*: Greenwood Guides to Historic Events, 1500-1990.

Fey, Linda and Frey, Marsha, eds. Westport, Connecticut: Greenwood Press, 2004.

Harran, Marilyn. *Luther on Conversion: The Early Years.* Ithaca, New York: Cornell University Press, 1993.

Heirich, M. T, "Change of Heart: A Test of Some Widely Help Theories About Religious Conversions," *American Journal of Sociology*, 83 (3), pp. 653-680, 1977.

Hill, Craig C. "Where Do We Go from Here," *Perspective Magazine: SMU Perkins School of Theology*, spring 2019, pp. 4-6.

Hindmarsh, Bruce. *The Evangelical Conversion Narrative: Spiritual Autobiography in Early Modern England*. Oxford: Oxford University Press, 2005.

Hollinghurst, Steve. *Mission Shaped Evangelism: The Gospel in Contemporary Culture*. Norwich: Canterbury Press, 2010.

Hunt, Earl. *Evangelism in a New Century*. Nashville: Discipleship Resources, 1996.

Hunter, James. *To Change the World: The Irony, Tragedy, and Possibility of Christianity in the Late Modern World*. Oxford: Oxford University Press, 2027.

James, Carolyn Custis. *The Gospel of Ruth: Loving God Enough to Break the Rules*. Grand Rapids: Zondervan, 2011.

Johnson, Ben. *Speaking of God: Evangelism as Initial Spiritual Guidance*. Louisville: Westminster Press, 1999.

Jung, L. Shannon. *Sharing Food: Christian Practices for Enjoyment*. Minneapolis: Fortress Press, 2008.

Kaiser, Kurt. *Chalice Hymnal*, no. 477, "Pass It On." Saint Louis: Chalice Press, 2003.

Kang, S.S. "The Church, Spiritual Formation, and the Kingdom of God: A Case for Canonical-Communion Formation Reading of the Bible," *Ex Auditu*, 18, 137-151.

Kennedy, James D. *Evangelism Explosion: Equipping Churches for Friendship, Evangelism, Discipleship, and Healthy Growth*. Carol Stream, Illinois: Tyndale House, 1997.

Killinger, John. *Outgrowing Church*. Eugene, Oregon: Wipl & Stock Press, 2019

Killinger, John. *The Changing Shape of Our Salvation*. New York: Crossroad Publishing Company, 2007.

Killinger, John. *The Zacchaeus Solution: How Christians Can Reverse the World's Economic Downturn*. Cleveland, Tennessee: Parson's Porch Books, 2010.

Kreider, Alan. *The Change of Conversion and the Origin of Christendom*. Eugene, Oregon: Wipf and Stock Publishers, 1999.

Krodel, Gottfried. *Christianity in Culture: A Study in Dynamic Theologizing in Cross-Cultural Perspective*. New York: Orbis Books, 1988.

Langer, Rob. "Points of Unease with the Spiritual Formation Movement," *Journal of Spiritual Formation and Soul Care*, 2012, pp 182-206.

Langford, Andy and William Willimon. *A New Connection: Reforming the United Methodist Church*. Nashville: Abingdon Press, 1998.

Leeming, David A. *Encyclopedia of Psychology and Religion*. Chennai, India: Mylapore Institute, 2019.

Leonard, Bill J. "Evangelism and Contemporary American Life," *Review & Expositor* 82, no. 4, 1980, pp. 493-507.

Lewis, C.S. *The Collected Letters of C.S. Lewis: Narnia, Cambridge, and Joy, 1950-1963, Vol. 3*. New York: Harper Collins, 2007.

Lewis, C.S. *The Weight of Glory and Other Addresses*. Grand Rapids: William B. Eerdmans, 1949.

Long, T.E. and J.K. Hadden. "Religious Conversion and the Concept of Socialization: Integrating the Brainwashing and Drift Models," *Journal for the Scientific Study of Religion*, 22 (1), pp. 1-14.

MacBeth, Sybil. *Praying in Color: Drawing a New Path to God*. Brewster, Massachusetts: Paraclete Press, 2007.

MacKintosh, H.R., *The Christian Experience of Forgiveness*. London: James Nisbet and Company, 1922.

MacMullen, Ramsey. *Christianizing the Roman Empire A.D. 100-400*. New Haven: Yale University Press, 1984.

Maddix, M. A. and R.P. Thompson. "Scripture as Formation: The Role of Scripture in Christian Formation," *Christian Education Journal*, 9, 79-93, 2012.

Malphurs, Aubrey. *Planting Growing Churches for the 21st Century*. Grand Rapids: Baker, 1998.

Matthews, Carl. "Remarks on the Theology of Joy," unpublished presentation presented at the Yale University Divinity School Center for Faith and Culture, New Haven, Connecticut, November 12, 2018.

McConnell, William T. *Renew Your Congregation: Healing the Sick, Raising the Dead.* Saint Louis: Chalice Press, 2007.

McGrath, Alister. *Reformation Thought: An Introduction*. Malden, Massachusetts: Blackwell Publishers, 2018.

McKnight, Scot. *Turning to Jesus: The Sociology of Conversion in the Gospels*. Louisville: John Knox Press, 2002.

McReynolds, James E. *Joy Comes in the Mourning: Love Is Forever*. Cleveland, Tennessee: Parson's Porch Books, 2020.

McReynolds, James E. *Dancing with God: A Theology of Joy*. Cleveland, Tennessee: Parson's Porch Books, 2016.

McReynolds, James E. *Spirit of Joy Church*. Cleveland, Tennessee: Parson's Porch Books, 2019.

McReynolds, James E. *The Joy of Preaching: Encountering Jesus Through the Word of God*. Cleveland, Tennessee: Parson's Porch Books, 2013.

McReynolds, James E. *The Joy of Prayer: The Way to Intimacy with God*. Cleveland, Tennessee: Parson's Porch Books, 2020

McReynolds, James E. *The Silence of the Church: The Spiritual Struggle with Sexuality*. Cleveland, Tennessee: Parson's Porch Books, 2017.

McReynolds, James E. *The Spirituality of Joy: The Least Discussed Human Emotion. Cleveland, Tennessee:* Parson's Porch Press, 2011.

Mead, L.B. *The Once and Future Church*. Washington, D.C.: Alban Institute, 1996.

Mead, Sydney. "The Rise of the Evangelical Conception of Ministry in America, 1607-1815," *The Ministry in Historical Perspectives*. New York: Harper and Brothers, 1960.

Morgan, Edmund. *Visible Saints: The History of the Puritan Idea*. Ithaca, New York: Cornell University Press, 1968.

Murray, Iain. *Revival and Revivalism: The Making and Marring of American Evangelicalism, 1750-1858*. Edinburgh: Banner of Truth, 1994.

Oates, Wayne. *Christ and Selfhood*. New York: Association Press, 1961.

Oberman, Heiko. *Luther: Man, Between God and the Devil*. New Haven: Yale University Press, 2006.

Olson, Roger. *The Story of Christian Theology: Twenty Centuries of Tradition and Reform*. Downers Grove: InterVarsity Press, 2002.

Osbeck, Kenneth W. *101 Hymn Stories: The Inspiring True Stories Behind Favorite Hymns*. Grand Rapids: Kregel Publications, 2013.

Palmer, J. T. *Education as Spiritual Formation*. New York: Educational Horizons, 005.

Paloutzian, R.F. "Religious Conversion and Spiritual Transformation: A Meaning- system Analysis," *Handbook of the Psychology of Religion and Spirituality*. New York: Guilford Press, 2005.

Peace, Richard. *Conversion in the New Testament: Paul and the Twelve*. Grand Rapids: William B. Eerdmans Publishing Company, 2001.

Peirce, Deborah. *A Scriptural Vindication of Female Preaching*. Carmel, New York: Burroughs, 1820.

Pierson, Robert. *Tell: How to Share Your Faith with Others*. Tulsa: Leadership Nexus, 2002.

Pippert, Rebecca. *Out of the Saltshaker and Into the World*. Downers Grove: InterVarsity Press, 2000.

Rambo, L.R. *Understanding Religious Conversion*. New Haven, Connecticut: Yale University Press, 1993.

Rauschenbusch, Walter. *A Rauschenbusch Reader*. New York: Harper & Brothers, 1957

Reed, A.H. *Quest for Spiritual Community: Reclaiming Spiritual Guidance for Contemporary Congregations*. New York T & T Clark International Publishers, 2010.

Reese, Martha Grace. *Unbinding the Gospel: Real Life Evangelism*. Saint Louis: Chalice Press, 2006.

Reynolds, William J. *Companion to the Baptist Hymnal*. Nashville: Broadman Press, 1976.

Reynolds, William J. *Hymns Today and Tomorrow*. Nashville: Abingdon Press, 1977.

Reynolds, William J. *Joyful Sound*. New York: Holt, Rinehart and Winston, 1978.

Robert, Dana Lee. *Evangelism at the Heart of Mission*. New York: United Methodist General Board of Global Missions, 1997.

Robertson, A. T. *Word Pictures in the New Testament*. Nashville: The Sunday School Board of the Southern Baptist Convention, 1930.

Sandage, S. J., Hill, P.C., Vaubel, D.C. "Relational Spirituality. Generativity, and Mental Health: Relationships and Pathways to Conversion," *The International Journal for the Psychology of Religion*, 21, 1-16, 2011.

Simpson, James. *Ordained to Ministry: Every Christian's Purpose for Being*. Cleveland, Tennessee: Pentecostal Institute of Church Growth, 1989.

Smith, Christian and Melinda Denton. *The Religious and Spiritual Lives of American Teenagers*. Oxford University Press, 2007.

Smith Gordon. *Beginning Well: Christian Conversion and Authentic Transformation.* Downers Grove: InterVarsity Press, 2014.

Southard, Samuel. *Pastoral Evangelism.* Nashville: Broadman Press, 1964.

Stark, Robert. *The Rise of Christianity: A Sociologist Reconsiders History.* Princeton, New Jersey: Princeton University Press, 2002.

Sweazey, George. *Effective Evangelism.* New York: Harper & Row, 1953.

Talbert, Charles H. *Reading Acts: A Literary and Theological Commentary on the Acts of the Apostles.* New York: Crossroad, 1997.

Tappert, Theodore G. ed. and trans. *Martin Luther: Letters of Spiritual Counsel. Library of Christian Classics.* Philadelphia: Westminster Press, 1955.

Turner, David. *Matthew.* Grand Rapids: Baker Academic Books, 2008.

Ullman, Carol. *The Transformed Self: The Psychology of Religious Conversion.* New York: Plenum Books, 1989.

Vaillant, G.W. *Spiritual Evolution: A Scientific Defense of Faith.* New York: Broadway Books, 2012.

Van Cappellen, Peter. "Rethinking Self-Transcendent Positive Emotions and Religion: Insights from Psychological and Biblical Research," *Psychology of Religion and Spirituality.* Minneapolis: Fortress Press, 2018.

Wallis, Jim. *The Call to Conversion.* San Francisco: Harper and Row, 1981.

Webber, Robert. *Ancient Future Evangelism: Making Your Church a Faith-Forming Community.* Grand Rapids: Baker Books, 2003.

Wesley, John. *The Works of John Wesley.* Los Angeles: Baker, 1996.

Willimon, William. *Rekindling the Flame: Strategies for a Vital United* Methodism. Nashville: Abingdon Press, 1987.

Witherington, Ben. *Troubled Waters: Rethinking the Theology of Baptism*. Waco, Texas: Baylor University Press, 2007.

Wood, D. R. W. and Howard, Marshall I. *New Bible Dictionary*. Leicester, England: InterVarsity Press, 1996.

Wriedt, Markus, "Luther's Theology," *The Cambridge Companion to Martin Luther*. Cambridge: Cambridge University Press, 2009.

Wright, N.T. *Justification: God's Plan and Paul's Vision*. Downers Grove: InterVarsity Press, 2009.

Wuthnow, R.D. *Sharing the Journey: Support Groups and America's New Quest for Community*. New York: Free Press, 1994.

Yancy, Philip. *What's So Amazing About Grace*. Grand Rapids: Zondervan, 1997.

Yohannan, K. P. *Revolution in World Missions*. Carrollton, Texas: International Standard Books, 2020 edition.

Yudell, Cliff. "Pastor, Evangelist, Crusader: Is Government Today a Religion Within Itself?" *Saturday Evening Post*, June 2005, pp. 2-3.

Zinnbauer, B.J. Spiritual Conversion: A Study of Religious Change Among College Students," *Journal for the Scientific Study of Religion*, 37, 161-180, 1998.

Notes about the Author

Dr. James McReynolds has shared Visionquests for Joy in more than a thousand places throughout the world. His books reveal new ways of doing evangelism. "Your preaching embraced with joy, will be, as my positive thinking, a fresh vision for communicating Christian faith. Jim, I anoint you minister of joy to the world," declared Norman Vincent Peale in a School of Practical Christianity in Pawling, New York.

His congregations received 20 gold and one silver medal for excellence in evangelism from the Holston Conference of the United Methodist Church. He also attained ten excellence in evangelism certificates from the Christian Church (Disciples of Christ) in the United States and Canada.

He has spoken in 105 high school baccalaureate occasions, 150 jail and prisons, more than 200 hospitals and medical centers, 5,300 campuses and on ten cruises on rivers and oceans.

During 70 years of serving as an ordained minister, he has devoted his life to teaching people how to create an atmosphere for joy that has revolutionized the lives of countless people. Dr. McReynolds served as a diplomat of the World Pastoral Care Center, the pastoral care committee of the Baptist World Alliance, and the prayer and spiritual formation task force of the Cooperative Baptist Fellowship.

Jim served as a public relations specialist for the Sunday School Board of the Southern Baptist Convention. He is now actively retired. Jim has been listed in *Who's Who in the South and Southwest*, *Who's Who in Health Care*, *Who's Who in Religion*, *Who's Who in the South and Southwest*, *Who's Who in America*, and *Who's Who in The World*.

He was given the honor of being an elite member of the Nebraska Navy as an admiral by the governor of Nebraska. This is an honor like a Kentucky Colonel. There is no ocean in Nebraska, but Jim has crossed the world's oceans multiple times.

Jim has earned nine academic degrees including five doctorates. He began his academic career at Carson-Newman University in Jefferson City, Tennessee. Baylor University in Waco Texas; Midwestern Theological Seminary, Kansas City, Missouri; the University of Missouri-Columbia

School of Journalism; Cardiff Theological College in London, England; Vanderbilt University Divinity School, Nashville, Tennessee; and the University of Oxford are among the esteemed institutions where he was educated in preparation to fulfilling his calling. His blend of scholarship and intensity for an experience allow the church to use the best of the past with enthusiasm for what the Spirit has mined deep into a vein of spiritual gold.

For the many people who have given up on the church, he brings a breath of fresh air. His wit and wisdom have resulted from Dr. McReynolds' decades of vulnerable ministry in the local church and the churches around the world. As a longtime friend since childhood noted, "Jim thinks theologically, but speaks and writes colloquially."

CONTACT INFORMATION VISIONQUESTS FOR JOY INTERNATIONAL

People search far and wide, some travel the whole planet for the feeling of pure joy. This anointed ministry for the kingdom started in a small way. Thousands of churches have been contacted with a goal of sharing times of joy. In times past, a few hundred letters would stimulate all the places needed for two years. Today sharing the Great Commission anywhere is not as easy. Contact the author to share a day, a weekend, a seminar, or any other speaking engagement. Dr. James McReynolds 320 North 4th Street Elmwood NE 68349 402-994-2370 phone joyminister@windstream.net

"Contemporary evangelism has overemphasized knowledge about God without leading people to experience God in ways that bring satisfying joy. We have a hollow husk of spirituality that has lost its heart, the joy of the Lord. My friend James McReynolds has created an apologetic for joy as a gift of that God gives us to inspire and renew. As you read his books or hear him preach, you will discover that the joys God gives are more deeply satisfying than you ever imagined."

-- Dr. Harold Bales, Davidson, North Carolina

"In the days God chose Jim to serve and envision the Great Commission, he has enjoyed the adventure of being an agent of God's kingdom. These days the Christian faith has become irrelevant. He sees connecting with a joyful God as what conversion means. Throughout many centuries since the Reformation, culture has created rigid rules and misdirected doctrines.

Jim's life is to focus on God whose radiant joy eclipses all else. The beauty of God takes away breath. The joy of God is the Source of a life-enriching relationship that converts us to changing our lives through the grace that never ends. I pray God will use me with the goal of helping God make joy a way of life for those who surrender to the Creator, who chose to have us live a life in these specific years of human history. "The writer's goal as a communicator is to lead people into the Word of God to become a faithful witness to the kind of life that flourishes eternally. The many books Jim has written on joy and life in the kingdom are filled with the joy of what God is doing. Surrendering to the Spirit, the joy of preaching, teaching, and writing is the way the Lord uses us all with all our gifts to know our small place in the Great Commission.

"What an awesome privilege it is to be alive as we enjoy the results of doing the Great Commission with every gift. Let us accept our weaknesses as well as the strengths."

-- Shana Shahid, Church of Pakistan

www.ingramcontent.com/pod-product-compliance
Lightning Source LLC
Chambersburg PA
CBHW072028110526
44592CB00012B/1435